WHEN
IN THE
ARAB
WORLD

WHEN IN THE ARAB WORLD

**An insider's guide to living and working
with Arab culture**

Rana F. Nejem

YARNU
Publications

First published in 2016 by Yarnu Publications
Amman,
Jordan
Telephone: +962 79 7661011
Email: Info@yarnu.com

ISBN 978-1-911195-20-7

Also available as an ebook

ISBN 978-1-911195-21-4

1 3 5 7 9 10 8 6 4 2

Typeset by Jill Sawyer Phypers

Cover design by Adpro Communications, Amman Jordan. Email: adpro@adprojo

Printed and bound by Clays Ltd, St Ives plc. United Kingdom

GRATEFUL FOR...

All the people who saw me through the journey of writing this book – all those who provided support, talked things over, read, offered comments, and assisted in the editing, proofreading and design.

I want to thank Alastair Campbell for planting the seed of the initial inspiration for this book. We both spoke at a conference in Sharjah in 2014, and when he heard me talk about some of the cross-cultural issues I examine in these pages, he said 'there is a book in all this if you can find time to write it.' As the author of so many books since he left Downing Street, his was a voice I felt was worth listening to, and in the subsequent weeks I began to sketch out a structure. I am grateful for that initial inspiration and his subsequent encouragement.

I want to thank everyone who gave of their time to be interviewed for this book to ensure that the reader does not only hear my voice but multiple voices of people from all over the world sharing their own personal experiences with the Arab culture. Some have asked me to change their real names, but their words remain their own. Thank you for helping me open my eyes to all the little but significant details that we consider normal but can cause so much confusion, stress and anxiety for many non-Arabs.

A special thank you to my dear friend Nissreen Haram for ensuring that I got all my facts right, without falling into the trap of making sweeping generalisations nor reinforcing prevailing stereotypes. Any inaccuracies or discrepancies remain my own responsibility.

A big thank you to the wonderful creative team at Adpro Communications in Jordan for doing a fantastic job with the cover design and for being so patient with my requests.

I would also like to acknowledge the work of three authors in particular who have written before me on this subject – Jeremy Williams; Dr. Jehad Al Omari and Margaret K. Nydell. Your excellent work served as a useful outline that helped me identify the gaps that still needed to be filled.

'Ask the experienced rather than the learned.'

A popular Arab proverb

CONTENTS

Introduction

WHY THIS BOOK?
Allow me to be clear up front: I am not a sociologist and this book is not an in-depth study of Arab culture; it is not about politics; and it is not a tourist guide, either.

This book is about breaking through the stereotypes and the misconceptions. It is about understanding the people and demystifying the culture of the Arab world, the beliefs, values and social structures that determine how business is conducted and how things are done.

Needless to say, inherent in writing this kind of book about the culture of such a large and diverse area is the difficulty of finding the balance between the 'general' and the 'specific', while not falling into the trap of oversimplifying matters. It hasn't been easy.

Of course there are differences between one Arab country and another – life in Beirut is vastly different from life in Riyadh. And there are differences within each country; between the capital city and the smaller cities. However, there are enough commonalities – the Arabic language, the Islamic religion, and in large parts, the Bedouin roots and values – that tie this vast region together, thereby justifying the generalisations that I make in parts of this book.

This is not a sterile list of dos and don'ts. My aim here is for you to walk away with a deeper knowledge and understanding of the motivators of behaviour, a wider perspective and a skill that will enable you to float with ease and confidence from one situation to the other. Only then will you be able to enjoy the wonderful journey of discovering those traditions that are unique to each place while building long-term fruitful relationships and successful enterprises.

But do not forget: we deal with *people*, not cultures. Each person is an individual with his or her own 'self-culture' – his or her own set of beliefs, values and viewpoints, which were formed as a result of personal experiences, upbringing, education and interactions with various other nations and cultures.

As an Arab myself, I had to make sure that I did not end up romanticising my own culture. Throughout writing this book I strived to be honest and authentic while taking care not to fall into the trap of replacing one set of stereotypes with another. To ensure that it remains a useful, practical guide, I have not relied solely on my perceptions and experiences but have included many interviews with business people, diplomats and expats from all over the world – Europe, the Americas, the Indian subcontinent, the Far East and even Australia – so that you could benefit from the experiences of people you may relate to from your own culture. In some cases, people have asked me to change their names, but their words remain their own.

WHO WOULD BENEFIT FROM THIS BOOK?

Everyone and anyone who wants to visit, or do business with, or live in the Arab world. Business executives at all levels, diplomats, government officials, students and, of course, the families and spouses who usually face the most difficulties when having to relocate to follow the career path of their family's breadwinner.

There is plenty of evidence to support the critical need for cross-cultural intelligence. How many a diplomatic crisis could have been avoided? How many broken business deals and fractured relationships could have been saved with a little cultural intelligence? Most of these problems are not the result of a wrong handshake or wearing inappropriate attire to a business meeting; these issues build up over time, causing confusion, frustration and even resentment.

CULTURE SHOCK

The online Oxford Dictionary defines culture shock as disorientation experienced when suddenly subjected to an unfamiliar culture or way of life.

When we move to a new country, everything is unfamiliar: the language, weather, food, dress code, values, beliefs and local customs, the way people interact, how business is conducted, and what is considered to be acceptable. Everything is different, and all these differences affect people in a variety of ways and degrees of intensity. Many people do not recognise what is bothering them. Reactions can start with surprise and develop into stress and feelings of disorientation, frustration, isolation and loneliness. For some, these feelings lead to relationship issues and conflicts with family, peers and colleagues. Anger and depression are very common emotions that come with culture shock, leading people to idealise their own culture while being extremely critical of the other culture: 'It is the people out there that cause the problems' or, 'Their system is so crooked.'

Too many people end up making wrong decisions in the midst of culture shock and, as a result, either pick up bad habits – such as overindulging in food, shopping or smoking – or terminate contracts and end up returning to their home country early, at a high financial cost for their businesses and organisations.

The best way to deal with culture shock is to learn as much as you can about the new country before you go, be open-minded and, once you get there, do not withdraw; build new relationships, go out, eat well, stay active and discover the country you are in and its people. And perhaps the most important piece of advice is to maintain a sense of humour and a light-hearted attitude.

WHAT IS CULTURE?

Many cross-cultural researchers and writers compare culture to an iceberg. Like an iceberg, culture has two distinct parts: one is visible above the waterline and the other is invisible under the waterline. Although the top part of the iceberg can be very interesting, almost 80 per cent of its mass is underwater. And it is in this hidden part that the foundations lie – the values, beliefs and all the underlying reasons why people behave the way they do.

Although technology, the media and ease of transportation continue to make the world smaller, and even unify us in certain ways, culture will never disappear. In fact, the more open the world is, the bigger the role of culture and the more important it is to be culturally intelligent.

The American anthropologist Edward T. Hall identified three different levels of culture: primary, secondary, and explicit or manifest. Hall saw *primary-level culture* as that in which the rules are known to all, obeyed by all, but seldom, if ever, stated. Its rules are implicit, taken for granted, and almost impossible for the average person to articulate as a system. *Secondary-level culture*, although known to everyone within that culture, is normally hidden from outsiders, but is as regular and binding as any other level of culture, possibly even more so. *Explicit* or *manifest culture* is what we all see and share; it is the façade presented to the world at large. However, because it is so easily manipulated, it is the least stable and least dependable for the purposes of decision-making.[1]

Several culturalists and sociologists have devised models to help us understand every culture in the world. Among those are the Lewis Model and the Three Colours of Worldview, first created by Roland Muller and further developed by Knowledgeworkx. I have tried to use some of these models as a framework for the different topics and information presented in this book. I will not go any further in explaining these models and theories and will leave it up to you to decide if you would like to pursue further reading in this field.

ACCEPTANCE IS KEY

The first step to cultural sensitivity is *acceptance*. It starts with understanding that there is no right and wrong – just different – and accepting that your way is just one of the options out there and that there are many different ways of seeing and doing things. As

---

1 Edward T. Hall, *The Dance of Life*, Anchor Books edition, 1989.

the philosopher David K. Naugle puts it: 'There is no impartial ground from which to reason or interpret reality.' Two people can be looking at the same picture, but they see completely different images. Different perceptions and different patterns of thinking will colour a person's view. Our brains play tricks on us, at times making us see things that are not even there and at other times allowing us to miss completely what is actually there. We draw conclusions because we are trained to see only certain things that are in line with our own perceptions, views and beliefs.

Cultural awareness is an ongoing process that starts with the commitment to maintain an open mind and a curious attitude that seeks to understand rather than judge. It requires that you first look inward at your own beliefs, viewpoints, behaviour and your own cultural traits – keeping in mind that while your society and traditions are the norm for you, they may appear strange to others.

Cultural intelligence is about learning to respond in a different manner that is appropriate to the context. It also requires a degree of emotional intelligence – in particular the ability to control feelings of anger, frustration and resentment, which are, in essence, fear of the unfamiliar. It doesn't mean that you must agree with the other's beliefs and viewpoints, and you are certainly not meant to shed your skin and change who you are. It involves adjusting the externals, like the lizard, but not changing the DNA.

> **Treat everyone as an individual**
>
> Cultural patterns are only guidelines; it doesn't mean that everyone you meet will behave in the same way. There are only tendencies and every person must be treated as an individual.

The point is to understand by focusing on the 'why' rather than the 'what' of what people do or don't do; to approach the experience with respect for the other mixed with genuine curiosity, rather than judgement and fear. This cannot be learned from a list of dos and don'ts. It takes time similar to the amount of time and effort you would invest getting started on a new job with a new organisation. You were hired for your skills, but you still need time to learn everything that is unique and specific to that organisation: the system, the rules, and how things are done there.

I EXPERIENCED IT FIRST HAND

My travels and work have shown me the value of a healthy dose of curiosity mixed with a willingness to look inwards and to question the long-lasting usefulness of some set beliefs and viewpoints. I learned to be more open-minded and accepting but, more importantly, I learned to control the default temptation to judge others for simply doing things in a way that I am not accustomed to. It hasn't been easy.

Now I teach inter-cultural intelligence and demonstrate to people from different cultures and backgrounds how essential it is to be a cultural learner in order to succeed in today's world. Still, I must admit, that even though I am so aware of this, I still sometimes find that I have to make a conscious effort to keep my fears and judgements at bay. It hit me again when I made my first business trip to the Kingdom of Saudi Arabia.

As an Arab having grown up in Kuwait and travelled many times to the UAE, Qatar and Oman, I'm very familiar with the culture of the Gulf states, but of course, Saudi Arabia is unique in many ways. I was very excited but also quite nervous as a woman travelling alone to Riyadh for the first time. I was quite surprised to find myself reverting back to my old – and I thought forgotten – conceptions. I had to consciously shift my attitude and switch on my curious cultural-learner perspective. In the end, I was very pleasantly surprised with the interactions I had while in Riyadh and the amazing Saudi women I had the pleasure of working with, who shattered some of the stereotypes that I – even as an Arab woman myself – carried in my mind.

As human beings, we tend to automatically judge and pigeonhole people so we can stay safe and comfortable in the familiar. I was reminded once again, that inter-cultural awareness is an ongoing process that requires a conscious effort and commitment, the results of which are well worth the effort invested.

My first experience of that was when I was working as a broadcast journalist for CNN during the First Gulf War. Daily we were faced with so many issues that were the result of simple misunderstandings or misinterpretations of culturally motivated behaviour. My colleagues took a lot of things for granted and applied what they believed to be universal standards of 'normal' and 'right'. Communication was a struggle. They could not see what I saw. It was as if we were looking at one of those pictures that had two images in them. I could see only one image while they were baffled and confused and could not see what I was talking about. I was so frustrated that I ended up taking a career-changing decision.

When I then moved to head the foreign press office at the Royal Hashemite Court, I invested a good part of my time speaking with Western journalists trying to get them to 'see' the underlying reasons why things are done the way they are and what is really important for us as Arabs and as Jordanians. In the process, I opened up my own mind and was able to see the fuller picture myself.

That experience came into play when I was advising British ambassadors and ministers in my capacity as head of the communications and public diplomacy department at the British Embassy in Amman. I advised diplomats, politicians and businesses on the best way to get their message across to an Arab audience, and on the most appropriate way to interact and build fruitful long-lasting relationships in the country and the region in general. Every single activity we did – whether it was the announcement of a business part-nership in the country, a royal visit, a political statement, or the launching of a project – everything had a 'cultural awareness' dimension to it. It was my responsibility to look at how a message could be understood or interpreted through a local lens and what could be done to ensure that no offence was committed and that we communicated the message that we actually intended to communicate.

It is mostly simple common sense, but it is extremely critical. It is the kind of thing that most people are unaware that they do not know. They therefore end up doing things the way they are used to doing them, simply because they cannot see there are other 'right' ways, and that what they see is not necessarily the full picture or the only picture.

In his book *Social Intelligence*, Daniel Goleman recounts an incident that took place during the early days of the second

American invasion of Iraq, which I think clearly demonstrates the crucial need for cultural and social intelligence.

A group of soldiers set out for a local mosque to contact the town's chief cleric. Their goal was to ask his help in organising the distribution of relief supplies. But a mob gathered, fearing the soldiers were coming to arrest their spiritual leader or destroy the mosque.

Hundreds of Iraqi Muslims surrounded the soldiers, waving their hands in the air and shouting as they pressed in toward the heavily armed platoon. The commanding officer, Lieutenant Colonel Christopher Hughes, thought fast. Picking up a loud-hailer, he told his soldiers to 'take a knee', meaning to kneel on one knee. Next he ordered them to point their rifles toward the ground. Then his order was: 'Smile.'

At that, the crowd's mood morphed. A few people were still yelling, but most were now smiling in return. A few patted the soldiers on the back, as their commander ordered them to walk slowly away backwards – still smiling.

That quick-witted move was the culmination of a dizzying array of split-second social calculations that perfectly hit the right gesture that would pierce the barriers of culture and language. That incident spotlights the brain's social brilliance even in a chaotic, tense encounter.[2]

---

2 Daniel Goleman, *Social Intelligence*, 2006 (Prologue).

UNINTENDED CONSEQUENCES

When I started doing interviews for this book, I came across so many stories of misunderstood signals that led to unintended consequences. One such incident happened with Alan, a strategy and communications consultant who was about to take up a major contract in one of the countries in the Arabian Gulf. The sheikh (a title used in the Gulf countries for members of the royal or ruling family) who heads the organisation that Alan was being hired to work with was on a working visit to the UK with another senior member of his staff; they asked to meet Alan to go over some details before finalising the contract. However, the only available day for them was a Sunday. Alan wasn't at all keen about disrupting his weekend, so he invited the sheikh and his manager over to his house for afternoon tea. They had their meeting and discussed the business that they needed to, and everyone seemed happy. What Alan hadn't realised is the meaning that the sheikh attached to being invited to Alan's home. For Arabs, it is an honour to be invited into someone's home. Especially in the Gulf countries, an invitation to someone's home is a signal that you are trusted and that the relationship has been taken to a higher level. While Alan was only thinking of convenience, his choice sent a more important – if completely unintended – signal to his Arab guests.

'YALLA'[3] ARE YOU READY?

Writing, researching and interviewing for this book has been an invaluable learning and fun experience for me. It has

---

3   Arabic word meaning 'come on, let's go'.

opened up my eyes to so many things that I had always taken for granted as 'normal'.

As you start on what I hope will be a very exciting journey of discovery for you, keep in mind that cultural patterns are only guidelines; they don't mean that everyone you meet will behave in the same way. There are only tendencies in a culture, and every person must be treated as an individual.

Arabs are a very generous people and are more than eager to help out when asked. So don't be afraid to ask for guidance, and you will find plenty of volunteers to help show you the right and most appropriate course of action for that particular situation and place.

WELCOME TO THE ARAB WORLD

Technology and the ease of travel have opened up the world, while globalisation has increased the mobility of people in search of better economic and social opportunities. Today, there are an estimated 244 million migrant workers around the world.[1] In the United Arab Emirates alone, 87 per cent of its population of nine million are expats.[2]

Straddling two continents, with 72 per cent of its territory in Africa and 28 per cent in Asia, the Arab world is one of the globe's most strategic regions. Historically known as the 'cradle of civilisation', it's where the world's earliest and culturally richest civilisations in history were founded, and where the three great monotheistic religions were born, later spreading to all corners of the world.

While Europe was plunged in its 'Dark Ages', the Arab and Islamic civilisation was at its peak – a beacon of learning and innovation, tolerance and trade. There was a time when the great cities of Baghdad, Damascus and Cairo took turns in providing invaluable contributions to science and

1 United Nations Population Fund, 2015 figures.

2 World Population Review, 2014.

literature that paved the way for the rise of the West to its present prominence.

Today, the Arab world – a rich blend of ethnicities and religions – is experiencing a wave of transformation and change, the results of which are still evolving. Still, one thing is certain: the abundance of opportunities, and the huge potential for growth and development that the region has to offer for entrepreneurs, investors and businesses, both large and small.

WHAT IS THE ARAB WORLD?

The Middle East and the Arab world are often confused as one and the same thing. They're not. The Middle East is a geographical area that is defined differently by various sources – sometimes stretching to include Iran and Pakistan and all of North Africa, and at other times stopping only at the Western border of Egypt.

The Arab world is made up of twenty-two countries that also make up the Arab League of Nations. The six nations that founded the Arab League in 1945 are: Egypt, Iraq, Jordan, Lebanon, Syria and Saudi Arabia, and the other nations that joined as they gained their independence are: Yemen, Libya, Sudan, Morocco, Tunisia, Kuwait, Algeria, the United Arab Emirates, Bahrain, Qatar, Oman, Mauritania, Somalia, Palestine, Djibouti and Comoros. They have a combined population of around 385.3 million[3] people, with over half under twenty-five years of age.

---

3   The World Bank Data website, 2014 figures.

Some would argue that not all people in those nations consider themselves Arab. In North Africa, for example, many Tunisians and Moroccans consider themselves distinctly Berber, not Arab, and some Lebanese consider themselves Phoenicians more than Arabs. Still, there remain enough commonalities – the Arabic language, religion, history and culture – that tie them with the rest of the Arab world.

There are a number of terms that are used throughout this book to describe various regions within the Arab world; **the Levant** refers to what Arabs have historically called Greater Syria, which includes Syria, Lebanon, Palestine and Jordan. **Al Maghreb Al Arabi** (the Arab West), which I also refer to as the North African Arab countries, are Morocco, Libya, Tunisia and Algeria. **The Arabian Peninsula** refers to Saudi Arabia, Yemen, Oman, Kuwait, the UAE, Qatar and Bahrain. Excluding Yemen, the countries of the Arabian Peninsula also make up the GCC (the Gulf Cooperation Council); I also sometimes refer to them as the Gulf countries.

THE ARABIAN GULF

To have a better understanding of the richness of Arab culture today, one must look at the influence and impact that other cultures have had historically over Arab culture, leaving their distinct traces on local traditions, architecture, cuisine and

The Arabian Gulf

There is a controversy regarding the name given to the Gulf, which shares a coastline with the non-Arab Iran in the north and east, and a number of Arab states to the West and south. It is sometimes referred to as the Persian Gulf. However, if you are in the Arab world you should refer to it as the Arabian Gulf.

even national costumes. In the Levant and Egypt, the Turkish influence from the Ottoman Empire remains strong, while the Persian influence is seen more in the Gulf countries, and the African is quite distinct in the Maghreb.

When the Ottoman Empire collapsed as a result of World War I, much of the Arab world fell under the control of the European colonial empires – France, Britain and Italy – which left their own mark on the local traditions of the countries they governed. Most Arab states only gained their independence during or after World War II: the Republic of Lebanon in 1943, the Syrian Arab Republic and the Hashemite Kingdom of Jordan in 1946, the Kingdom of Libya[4] in 1951, the Kingdom of Egypt[5] in 1952, the Kingdom of Morocco and Tunisia in 1956, the Republic of Iraq in 1958, Algeria in 1962, and the United Arab Emirates in 1971. Saudi Arabia was unified under Ibn Saud of Saudi Arabia by 1932. Oman, apart from brief intermittent Persian and Portuguese rule, has been self-governing since the eighth century.

Within the Arab world there remain a number of ethnicities that have maintained their own separate identity and culture while being part of the Arab world. These are:

- **Kurds**, the majority of whom live in the northern regions of Iraq and Syria. They are an Indo-European ethnic group who speak Kurdish, a language close to Persian.

---

4   Libya was a kingdom until September 1969 when Muammar Qaddafi staged a military coup, launching the Libyan Revolution.

5   Following the revolution by the Free Officers Movement, in June 1953 the Egyptian Republic was declared.

The majority of Kurds are Muslim, with a small Christian minority. The aspiration for an independent state of Kurdistan has created conflict between the Kurdish minorities and their governments in Iraq, Iran, Syria and Turkey.

- **Amazigh,** the indigenous population of North Africa, who are also referred to as Berber. They do not speak Arabic (they speak Amazigh) and their numbers are largest in Morocco and Algeria. Government worries about separatist movements have created tensions; however, now in both Morocco and Algeria the Amazigh languages are being taught in schools and universities.

- **Armenians,** who migrated to the Arab world after the 1915 genocide. They live mostly in Lebanon, Syria and Jordan and in lesser numbers in Egypt and Iraq. They are Christians following the Orthodox Armenian Church.

- **Circassians**, who originate from the North Caucasus. They are predominantly Muslim, and currently live in Iraq, Syria, Jordan and Lebanon in relatively small numbers.

OIL AND GOD
The Arab world has unfortunately become infamous for either its opulent oil wealth or the religious fanatical groups that have hijacked and distorted realities in this part of the world.

Since discovering large deposits of petroleum in the 1930s, Saudi Arabia, Iraq, the UAE, Kuwait and Qatar have become among the top ten petroleum- and gas-exporting countries in the world. Smaller but significant reserves in the Arab world are also found in Algeria, Libya, Syria, Bahrain, Egypt, Tunisia and Sudan.

Although most of the Arab states are still developing economies, many have decided to diversify their economic base and have developed various industries. Still, the region's biggest economic challenge remains job creation for its youthful and growing population. The Arab World Competitiveness Report of 2013[6] identified a number of barriers to job creation and private-sector expansion, which differ across the region, 'with weak institutions and labour markets singled out as the most significant areas for improvement in North Africa; weak infrastructure and institutions in the Levant; and a pervasive education and innovation gap in countries in the Gulf'.

THE ARAB SPRING

The 'Arab Spring' is a term that was created and made popular by the Western media in early 2011 to describe the wave of anti-government protests that swept across several Arab states following the successful uprising in Tunisia that brought down Zine El Abidine bin Ali.

The Arab Spring is not one thing. Unlike what happened in Communist Eastern Europe in 1989 after the fall of the Berlin Wall, each affected Arab country has moved in a different and sometimes opposing direction. While Arab populations called for change, there was no consensus on the political and economic model that should replace existing regimes. In

6   A report published by the World Economic Forum in collaboration with the European Bank for Reconstruction and Development (EBRD).

some of these countries protesters wanted to reform the system under their current rulers, while others wanted to overthrow their leaders but did not have a clear view of what they wanted post free elections. While calls for greater social justice were strong, some were happy with gradual reforms but few had any magical solutions for their economies. On the other hand, leftist groups were pulling towards the reversal of privatisation deals, while others were pulling for more liberal reforms to allow the private sector to grow. Among the many voices were those of Islamist extremist groups that were well funded, well trained and had extensive networks in their respective countries.

At the time of writing this book, the jury was still out on whether the so-called Arab Spring uprisings had succeeded or failed – Tunisia is looking like a success story, Egypt has found some sort of order, while Syria, Libya and Yemen are still embroiled in violence; transformations are still ongoing and the outcome is far from clear. Nonetheless, many agree that 'the main legacy of the Arab Spring is in smashing the myth of the Arabs' political passivity and the perceived invincibility of arrogant ruling elites'.[7]

TERRORISM

Nothing has created more of a rift between the Arabs and the West than the issue of terrorism. In the aftermath of the 11 September 2001 terrorist attacks on the US, the threat of militant terrorist groups that have hijacked Islam has taken centre stage worldwide. While these extremely violent religious

---

7   Primoz Manfreda, researcher and political risk analyst for the Middle Eastern region.

extremists represent a minority view, their threat is real – not only to the West but also to the Muslim populations of the Arab world.

Hamas and Hezbollah

Although Hamas and Hezbollah are considered terrorist organisations by some countries, the vast majority of Arabs see them as political groups that are fighting a legitimate war against the Israeli occupation.

I am not going to get into an explanation of the various militant groups and their objectives, nor am I getting into the debate of the causes and drivers of terrorism. That is a complicated subject that I choose to leave for the specialised political and social scientists. My aim here is to give you a general overview of the Arab perspective on the subject so that you could be better prepared when entering conversations with your Arab associates, counterparts and even friends.

Concern about Islamic extremism is high and growing among people in the region. A survey by the Pew Research Centre[8] shows that 92 per cent of people in Lebanon are worried about Islamic extremism, while eight in ten in Tunisia, and six in ten in Jordan are anxious about the rise of extremism.

The most brutal and horrific of these militant groups is the Islamic State – also known as *Da'esh* in Arabic – which has succeeded in taking over large chunks of land in Syria and Iraq.

---

8   Pew Research Centre, spring 2014, Global Attitudes Survey.

When in the Arab world, you will hear strong arguments that these murderers have nothing to do with Islam, that they are a threat to the safety and security of the Arab countries, and that they were created by the United States' foreign policies and interference in the Arab world. You will also hear that the Arabs do not hate the American people; on the contrary, there

> **Views of ISIS overwhelmingly negative**
>
> Ninety-nine per cent of Lebanese and 94 per cent of Jordanians surveyed in 2015 were strongly opposed to ISIS.[9] (Exact figures are not available for other Arab countries.)

is an interest that borders on fascination with the way things are done in the US. But you will also hear strong concerns about the Western governments' policies that are perceived to be blatant attempts to break up the Arab world and control its resources. You will hear from the younger generation how open they are to the world and how eager they are to learn, grow and build successful enterprises. And you will also hear from their parents, who saw their dreams of Arab unity shattered, who are trying to hold on to their traditions and roots while everything around them is in turmoil. The truth of the matter is that the Arabs are not interested in changing any other country's way of life; they just don't want anyone to change theirs.

It is true that the likes of Osama Bin Laden, Abu Sayyaf and the horrific ISIS carry the bulk of the responsibility for tarnishing the image of the Arabs and Islamic culture; nevertheless, Western media and Hollywood have, too, contributed to

---

9   Pew Research Centre survey, November 2015.

the damage. Arabs are almost always portrayed as either evil terrorists threatening the civilised and free world, or ignorant, wealthy sheikhs squandering their wealth on frivolous life-styles. Rarely do we hear about the great achievements, the significant breakthroughs and the worthy innovations.

THE WAR ON IRAQ

It is no secret that the vast majority of Arab governments share the view of their public that the US-led war on Iraq was the result of bad judgement – the devastating regional conse-quences of which are still unfolding.

The 2003 US invasion and subsequent occupation of Iraq destroyed the country's national identity and replaced it with smaller sectarian and ethnic identities. The lack of security in the years that followed the invasion of Iraq resulted in one of the largest ethnic and sectarian cleansing campaigns in the region's history.

So if you were to ask any Arab about Iraq, the simplified answer you would most likely hear would be something along the lines of: 'Before 2003 Iraq was a thriving country, where millions went to work and had their basic needs satisfied, even though they could not express their political views. And today, they still cannot express their political views, but they've also lost their livelihoods, their security and their basic needs.'

THE ARAB-ISRAELI CONFLICT

You cannot go to the Arab world without knowing at least the basics of one of the biggest, still unresolved, global geopolitical conflicts. The establishment of the State of Israel in 1948 in Palestine gave rise to the Arab–Israeli conflict, which has occupied politicians, negotiators and mediators for over six decades and claimed over 120,000 lives, the vast majority of which were Palestinians. As is the case in most conflicts, even the facts can change, depending on which side you are on and where you are standing. There is, however, one unquestionable fact, namely that Israel is the only remaining occupying country in the world.

The socio-economic consequences of this protracted and still ongoing conflict are felt in many aspects of life in the Arab world and are a major factor affecting the ideologies of political movements and policies of governments in the Arab world.

Peace agreements were signed between Israel and Egypt in 1979, and Israel and Jordan in 1994, which have resulted in very cold and tense relations, while the interim Oslo Accords led to the creation of the Palestinian National Authority in 1994. On 29 November 2012, the UN General Assembly overwhelmingly[10] approved the de facto recognition of a sovereign Palestinian state. Although politically this resolution was extremely significant, it did little to change the sad reality on the ground.

Estimates vary of the number of Palestinian refugees displaced in 1948 from within what became the borders of Israel, and in 1967 during the subsequent Six-Day War. Today UNRWA[11] provides its services to over five million Palestinian

---

10   138 voted in favour, 9 against and 41 abstained.

11   The United Nations Relief and Works Agency, which was established in 1950 to

refugees who live in refugee camps in Jordan, Lebanon, Syria, the Gaza Strip and the West Bank, including East Jerusalem.

The Key

When the Palestinian refugees of 1948 and 1967 left their homes, they took their keys with them in their belief that their return was imminent. The keys have been passed on from generation to generation as a memory of their lost homes and as lasting symbols of their desired 'right of return'.

The conditions of Palestinians in the Arab world vary widely. According to the Palestinian Refugee Research Net[12], most Palestinians living in Jordan are full citizens, and enjoy a standard of living generally equivalent to other Jordanians. Fewer than one in eight Palestinian refugees in Jordan lives in a camp, and most camps have effectively become urban neighbourhoods.

Before the conflict in Syria, Palestinian refugees were non-citizens, but were provided with full access to employment and social services.

Conversely, stateless Palestinians in Lebanon face numerous employment restrictions and are barred from owning property. Consequently, they generally live in adverse circumstances, often in poor and overcrowded refugee camps. Because of this, many have left the country, and the actual number of refugees in Lebanon is likely much lower than

respond to the needs of the Palestinian refugees.

12   PRRN is a non-partisan project devoted to the dissemination of ideas and scholarly information. It is maintained by the Inter-University Consortium for Arab and Middle Eastern Studies (Montreal), with the support of the Arts Computing Network, McGill University and the International Development Research Centre.

UNRWA figures. Reforms and some minor changes to the employment policy were introduced in 2005.

In Kuwait, most Palestinians fled or were forced to leave after the 1990–91 Gulf War. In 1995, Libya expelled many of its Palestinians in a bizarre protest against the peace process. In Iraq, many refugees faced attacks after 2003, and fled the country. In Egypt and the Gulf states, Palestinians are typically treated as foreign visitors or foreign residents.

A final settlement to the Israeli-Palestinian conflict has yet to be reached and a peace process (referred to by some journalists as the MEPP) is still ongoing.

WHAT I KNOW NOW AND WISH I KNEW THEN

While writing this book, I met and interviewed a number of expats from all over the world who work, or have worked, in various Arab countries. I asked them what their experience in the region had taught them and what they wished they knew when they first arrived.

Giovanna Negretti, who is from Puerto Rico and works with civil society: 'That culture and religion are two different things. A lot of things that I thought came from the religion were actually cultural and had nothing to do with the religion.'

Chen Yi Xuan, a Chinese teacher: 'How important it is to be patient and to accept that the standard of efficiency here is very different.'

Peter Millett, who is British, also stressed the importance of being patient and resilient, but he also wished he knew 'how enormously important respect and honour were in the Arab world'.

Alexis McGinness, an American working in the field of development, wishes she had known the importance of family and how much people's lives here revolve around the family: 'It is something that plays into so many dynamics; it affects the way people work as well as social expectations.'

Eric, a management consultant from Sweden thought the region would be quite behind in its development and that business practices would be less sophisticated: 'I had not been aware how well educated the leaders are across the region. People are well informed and most people have been exposed to travelling and living outside the region. I find there is a great deal of curiosity here. There is an enormous passion to learn, to do the right thing, to develop. The commitment to build a prosperous society is huge; I find that quite admirable.'

James Thomas a corporate culture specialist from the UK: 'Understanding the background of motivators and influences that you do not see. Now I understand the significance of personal positioning, politicking and reputation and the impact that has on risk averseness. Now I understand the importance of that and why people might make decisions that are not purely based on what is clearly the right commercial decision to make.'

Tony Goldner, an Australian who has been doing consultancy work with various governments in the region since 2006:

'That this culture is all about keeping things in balance, and how much people would do to avoid conflict. I had to work hard on moderating my own communication style and the way I express my thoughts, which was too direct for this culture.'

Tari Lang, a communications and leadership advisor from Indonesia: 'That blurring between work and friendship in the Middle East. The very close relationship between doing business and having personal engagement in the Arab world. I found it very fulfilling and I love working here; even with all the frustrations I do love it because you do feel that things can move forward quite effectively.'

Toshihiro Abe, vice president of a large supplier of automotive parts: 'Japan is so far away from the Arab world, the only thing I knew about Arabs before coming here was four wives and killing people. Once I understood the Arab people I found them really wonderful; they respect relationships and they are not just thinking about business and profit. It is very sad for me to see how the Japanese people view the Arabs. If we know more, we would be much closer.'

David, a diplomat who arrived in the region in 2007, perceived the Arab world as a very hostile place: 'How warm the people in the Arab world can be. I came with a bit of a defensive mentality, I wanted to engage and to get to know people but I was a bit anxious about it. I thought they would have a hostile view of us because they hate the invasion of Iraq. But I found that in every place, people in the Arab world are unbelievably generous, open and warm; even if they hate your country's policy, they love getting to know you as a human being.'

Dan Monaghan, a retail commercial manager from the UK: 'I wish I knew how welcoming everyone is here. When I go back home, I always tell everybody: you cannot really understand what the Arab mentality means until you go there and experience what true hospitality is about and how you treat your guests, and how you treat new people that come into your life. I have never felt so welcomed anywhere else I go.'

SOCIETY IN THE ARAB WORLD

The early Arabs of the Arabian Peninsula were predominantly nomads – or Bedouins – who herded their sheep, goats and camels through the harsh desert. Where they found water in the oases, they settled and planted dates and cereals. Their settlements served as trade centres for the caravans transporting the spices, ivory and gold of southern Arabia and the Horn of Africa to the civilisations further north.[1]

Although today it is closely identified with Islam, the Arab identity was defined and recognised independently of religion, with historical records of Arab Christian kingdoms and Arab Jewish tribes predating the spread of Islam.[2] When Islam arose from the Arabian Peninsula in the early seventh century, the religion united the Bedouins with the town dwellers of the oases, and the language of the Holy Quran, Arabic, became the language of much of the Middle East and North Africa. Today, most Arabs are Muslim (Sunni, Shia), with a minority of Arabs of other faiths, largely Christian, but also Druze and Bahai.

---

1 *Encyclopaedia Britannica.*

2 Ori Stendel, *The Arabs in Palestine*, Sussex Academic Press, 1996.

Urbanisation, industrialisation and Western influences have over the centuries modified and changed traditional Arab values. The majority of Arabs today live in cities and towns where family and tribal ties are slowly eroding.

THE FAMILY AND TRIBE: A SOCIAL FORCE

The key to understanding the motivators of behaviour in Arab culture is to understand the power and pivotal importance of the family, honour and dignity. And by family here, I don't just mean the nuclear family but the larger extended family.

Although Arab societies have developed and modernised over the years, the tribal culture in most, but not all, of the Arab countries continues to have a strong influence on the structure of society and many of its values and beliefs. The veneer may be misleading to the outsider, who sees the high-rise buildings, the high-tech offices, the people who look quite modern and Westernised – yet the underlying base is a strong social cohesion rooted in the tribal traditions.

These tribal beliefs and traditions manifest themselves in different areas of life in Arab society. For example, the Bedouin or nomadic lifestyle required a lot of heavy physical work and many tasks had to be completed simultaneously. Therefore, families had to

The attitude towards older people

Age in the Arab world is respected and regarded as wisdom and experience. Elders are treated with deference and are looked after by their family. The concept of old people's homes is completely rejected and seen as a sign of Westernisation and lack of compassion.

be large for practical reasons, the first of which is that children aid in labour. Because family members are believed to be more committed to the common interests of the tribe and can be trusted more than hired hands, a man had to produce a lot of children.

Large families also enhance political stature. The factor that determined military strength before the Arab states gained their independence was the number of fighters an individual could muster. The man who could call on five or six adult sons and a similar number of sons-in-law to support him was a force with which to be reckoned. Cultural values underline this emphasis on offspring. A man is not a man if he cannot produce children, and a woman is not really an adult if she does not become a mother.

Sons and daughters

A son remains the most valued among the offspring in Arab families. A son carries the family name and inherits the family's wealth. Although Arabs do honour and love their daughters, a boy enjoys a special elevated status within his family.[3]

Today the extended family is both a political and social force and an entire support system. It is a close-knit structure where the patriarch is the head of the family and elders are revered and looked after. Members of the same extended family, clan or tribe stand up for each other during difficult times. The responsibilities and the decisions are shared, since any wrongdoing brings shame to the entire family, whose name the individual carries. For someone from North America or northern Europe, this may seem a bit too close for

---

3   See also 'Names, titles and forms of address', page 149.

comfort, however, Jonghee Son, a businesswoman who works in the travel and tourism sector, found some similarities with her own South Korean culture: 'For us, too, respect for elders and very strong family ties are very important, but maybe not so much for the bigger extended family.'

The resulting social structure is that young men and women continue to live in the family home with their parents until they get married, no matter how old one is. It is very common that a son would get married and live in the same building as his parents. A working woman leaves her young children with her mother or mother-in-law to look after while she is at the office. And Friday (the weekend across the Arab world except for Lebanon and Tunis) is usually spent visiting the extended family.

Dating and arranged marriages

Don't allow the outward signs of growing liberalisation in certain segments of Arab society to deceive you. The majority of Arab societies remain very conservative and will not allow the Western concept of dating. Arranged marriages are still common where the girl is allowed to meet her soon to be husband under the supervision of a chaperon from her family.

However, these rules are shunned by some of the elite in the more Westernised capital cities – such as Beirut, West Amman and Tunis, where the younger generation continues to push boundaries and challenge these traditions.

FAMILY AND BUSINESS

To do business in the Arab world you must understand that loyalty to the family comes before all other social relationships, even business.

Children are taught who is who, not just today, but also in history. So they grow up listening to stories about people in their family and tribe, and their relationships to other families and tribes. History is very important. Children learn that they wouldn't be where they are today if it wasn't for their fathers and their fathers' fathers before them.

Sally Zhang, a businesswoman, found this aspect similar to her own Chinese culture: 'Family relations are very close in China too, and when the father has a business he works very hard to grow that business, to then give it to his sons and then his grandchildren.'

'I quickly learned that even in Lebanon, one of the most open Arab cultures, the family is central,' Graham Ball, an independent business consultant who has spent a number of years living and working in Beirut says. 'Many businesses are still family owned, so criticism of family members, even if richly deserved, is not wise in virtually all cases. As a new employee, even in a senior capacity, when family are involved, expect to be excluded from all important decisions, until you have had time to build that all-important personal relationship and gained their trust.'

THE FAMILY IS PRIVATE
Asking about someone's wife and family, even when you don't know them, is considered a polite and harmless way of engaging in small talk in Western culture. This, however, is considered inappropriate in the Middle East and can easily cause offence.

Stephen, the CEO of a large property-development company based in the US, had just returned from his third visit to Cairo when I met him. He could not work out the reason this particular contract with a major client in Cairo suddenly went cold. 'Everything seemed to be going really well. We are the best company for the project and any competition is far behind. I thought I hit it off really well with my Egyptian counterpart. A really nice gentleman by the name of Ibrahim, who was educated in the West and speaks very fluent English. I don't understand why he has changed his attitude towards me. I don't see how I could have offended him.'

After going into more details about their numerous encounters, it turned out that Stephen was briefly introduced to Ibrahim's wife at an official function. The next time Stephen saw Ibrahim he did what he thought was the polite thing to do, according to his own cultural values, and asked Ibrahim: 'How is your lovely wife? You are one lucky man.' Stephen failed to read the signals from Ibrahim when the man did not reply, and went on to ask: 'So how long have you two been married?'

That, I explained to Stephen, was the proverbial nail in the coffin of that relationship. The family in Arab culture remains private, and asking about any female relatives is considered very inappropriate and could be interpreted – in more conservative societies – as an affront to the man's honour. What Stephen should have done in that situation is to completely refrain from mentioning the wife and simply ask about the children and the family in general.

Socialising with the opposite sex

In the countries of the Levant as well as in Egypt and the Maghreb countries, it is normal and acceptable for the sexes to mix publicly in restaurants and cafés. However, this is not the case for Gulf nationals in their countries, where unmarried couples or friends would not feel comfortable socialising in public places. Many restaurants are divided into sections for 'families' and another for men on their own. So it is common to see tables with groups of men out on their own and separate tables with groups of women on their own.

The social rules for non-Arabs are more lax, but you must never forget the overall conservative nature of Arab culture, which varies in strictness from one country to the other. Public displays of affection – kissing, hugging and in many cases even holding hands – is totally unacceptable across the Arab world and in some countries can lead to legal punishment.

THE FAMILY AND TRIBE: A POLITICAL FORCE

The maturity and strength of political parties differ from country to country in the Middle East. In many countries the extended family, clan or tribe continues to take the place of a political party. In countries such as Jordan and Kuwait, people run for parliamentary elections based on their tribal or family name and only after they have received the backing of the tribe.

The patriarchal nature of Arab society also reflects on the nature of the relationship between the people and their rulers and governments. Traditionally, people saw the ruler as the patriarch solely responsible for providing them with all their needs – a comfortable government job, education and healthcare for them and their families.

WHAT IS A *JAHA*?

A tribal tradition, a *Jaha* consists of the elders and leaders of a tribe that come together for a purpose – either to meet the *Jaha* of another tribe to ask for a girl's hand in marriage for one of their sons, or to resolve a dispute between people or families of the same tribe or of different tribes. It may sound archaic, but it is still the norm in most Arab countries.

British Ambassador Peter Millett talks of his experience and how he hadn't realised how important these tribal traditions were. 'Within the first two weeks of my arrival in Jordan, I was asked to be a part of a *Jaha*; a young British man was getting engaged to a Jordanian girl, so the bridegroom wanted me, as his "tribal leader", to be there. For me, learning how to go through the greeting line, how the tribal leaders sit across from each other while the top person speaks and then the Arabic coffee is served as a sign of closing the deal – it was all a good demonstration for me of the strongly traditional nature of Jordanian and Arab society.'

A *Jaha* is also essential for resolving very serious disputes. A British businessman living and working in Jordan was driving his car from Amman up to the north of Jordan; he accidentally hit an older man who was crossing the main highway after his car broke down on the side of the road. The pedestrian was seriously injured. The British business-man understood the local sensitivities and immediately sought advice regarding the tribal laws of the country. I was working at the British Embassy at the time and provided cultural advice on the best way to handle the situation. A *Jaha* was arranged, and representatives of the man who was driving the car joined the *Jaha* and paid their respects and condolences to the family of the deceased, expressing the driver's remorse over the accident. Only then did the family of the deceased drop charges against the driver.

THE GENERATION GAP

The gap between generation X and generation Y in the Arab world is probably greater and more evident than in many other cultures. The younger generation of Arabs have been well educated in some of the top universities in the US and Europe. They are savvy, well-travelled and exposed to the world much more than the majority of their generation in the West.

Drawn more to international corporate business standards, this generation doesn't want to be told what to do. They want to be challenged, they want to find their own solutions, they want value and meaning from the jobs they have and do not necessarily attach the same weight to their elders' values, beliefs and traditions.

LGBT rights

Same-sex relationships are illegal in Libya, Morocco, Sudan, Tunisia, Algeria, Kuwait, Oman, Saudi Arabia, Syria, UAE and Yemen. Punishment varies from fines and two years' imprisonment up to seventeen years' imprisonment.

While same-sex relationships are not explicitly illegal in the other Arab countries (such as Egypt and Jordan), they are still considered un-Islamic and can be punishable through some broadly written morality laws. Discretion is key.

WOMEN IN ARAB SOCIETY

The progress that Arab women have carved out for themselves since they resolved to change their circumstances decades ago has exceeded what many believed possible. And when the winds of change blew over the region in 2011, Arab women fought bravely to demand dignity and new freedoms for themselves and their families.

Today, women across the Arab world have broken traditional taboos and made significant achievements in every area and sphere of life. Today's Arab women and girls are healthier, better educated and more financially productive than ever before. Women across the Arab world have emerged among the leaders in every field – politics, business and science – and even in some of the conservative Gulf states women are cabinet ministers, parliamentarians, senators and ambassadors, surgeons, pilots, engineers, bankers and CEOs of major companies.

Still, there are many who remain bound by their families and the patriarchal nature of the society. Male dominance is ingrained in Arab culture – which leaves women, to a large extent, socially subordinate. The male is the head of the family and makes the decisions – whether he is the father, husband or brother.

The wider debate on women's rights continues to rage across the Middle East, with conservative voices on the one hand questioning the motives and hidden agenda behind women's rights movements: Are Arab feminists merely imitating women's liberation movements in the West? Is there a hidden agenda to destroy the Arab family? Do demands for women's rights seek to undermine religion?

Four wives

Polygamy in Islam is not a rule but rather an exception, and not very common today. Viewed in its historical context, it was the only way for a widowed woman whose husband was killed in battle to get protection for herself and her orphaned children.

Before the Quran was revealed, there was no upper limit for polygamy and many men had scores of wives. Islam puts an upper limit of four wives and gives a man permission to marry two, three or four women, only on the condition that he deals with them justly. In the same chapter, Surah Nisa, verse 129, it says: 'It is very difficult to be just and fair between women.'

On the other hand, Arab champions of women's rights – both male and female – find women's rights both compatible with Islam and in keeping with their own history. People are slowly realising that creating opportunities for women will not affect the culture's Islamic values, nor will it threaten to change the core traditional ways of society.

The whole topic of women's rights and gender equality is fraught with so many cultural issues. I would like to warn you here against falling into the stereotype trap and the assumption that women who do not drive or women who wear the veil are somehow oppressed, and will 'see the light' once they learn more about Western gender equality.

The concept of 'personal freedom' or 'the freedom to choose' is a Western cultural belief, and is central to the way of life in many nations. However, other cultures, including Arab culture, place more value on identification with one's place and role in society. This is what Brooks Peterson, who helps people from different cultures work together, called 'the freedom versus identity continuum',[4] and is important to keep in mind while interacting with people from different cultures, especially on the complicated issues related to gender equality.

The Tunisian experience

The Tunisian experience remains a model among the Arab states. Half a century has passed since the issuing of the Personal Status Code, through which Tunisian law gave legal effect to the principle of women's equality with men. The Code continues to develop through the application of original legal thinking to keep it in step with changing issues in Tunisian society[5].

At the time I was writing this book, King Abdullah of Saudi Arabia passed away, and President Obama and his wife Michelle were among the many heads of state who visited Riyadh to pay condolences to the new king. What Mrs Obama decided to wear – or not to wear – on that very high-profile diplomatic visit created a huge uproar on social media and various international and US news outlets. The US media applauded Michelle's decision not to cover her hair, and saw it as 'a defiant move in support of Arab women's human rights'. This episode was a stark example of the West getting it all wrong.

Michelle Obama, in my opinion, was ill advised and her appearance showed a lack of social and cultural intelligence

---

4   Brooks Peterson, *Cultural Intelligence: A Guide to Working with People from Other Cultures*, Intercultural Press, 2004, page 133.

5   UNDP, *The Arab Human Development Report*, 2009

and respect for the culture of the country she was visiting and the solemnness of the occasion of that visit. It is *not* about the veil – as foreign women are not required to wear the headscarf in Saudi Arabia – although she would have communicated a lot of awareness and respect had she worn a loose veil in the same way she did when she visited the Vatican (as did Queen Rania of Jordan when she visited the Vatican). The issue was more about her choice of clothes. Black and white is the colour worn for funerals in the Arab world,[6] yet the First Lady of the United States chose to wear a blue top and a patterned white and blue long jacket that would have been more suited for a casual lunch somewhere else, totally oblivious of the message that she was sending to her hosts and the offence she was causing.

But the point that really hit me when reading all the media coverage was how the headscarf, or the veil, is viewed by the West, and how it is assumed that Muslim and Arab women who wear the hijab[7] are oppressed and need someone to protect their human rights and free them from the 'tyranny of the veil'.

Freedom, right and wrong, honour and shame are not universal concepts. They mean different things to different people and carry completely different references in different cultures. Please do not fall into that trap and do not rush to make assumptions about Arab women and what they need based on your own cultural beliefs and values. I hope this book will help.

Businesswoman Jonghee Son's impression is a point in case: 'Women in the Arab world have much better rights than in

---

6 See 'Funerals', page 188.

7 See also 'Appearance and dress codes', page 156.

Korea. I know a lot of families here where the woman controls everything, she is like the Interior Minister: you have to listen to her.'

WOMEN IN THE WORKPLACE

Women across the Arab world have made major strides in the workplace, although studies show that female labour participation in the Arab world is quite low – especially when compared with the level of economic development in these Arab countries. World Bank Group research[8] concludes that the explanation for this could reside in the nature of economic growth and gender norms in the Arab world. The study states that economic growth in the area has not been labour-intensive, has generated few jobs, and has not been in female-friendly sectors, resulting in weak demand for women in the workforce, especially urban, educated women. And when men and women compete for scarce jobs, men may have priority access because of employers' and households' preferences.

On the other hand, research published by management consultants McKinsey has found that gender diversity is gaining a place on the corporate agenda across the Gulf countries in particular, as companies there increasingly recognise the potential of women leaders to enhance organisational effectiveness.[9]

However, the challenges remain big and the barriers tangible in practical terms. For instance, in Saudi Arabia, which is

---

8 *Female Labour Participation in the Arab World*, Policy Research Working Paper, World Bank Group, Poverty Global Practice Group, September 2014.

9 McKinsey report, *GCC Women in Leadership – from the first to the norm*, July 2014.

the largest labour market in the region, local companies are requested to build separate working areas and support spaces for female employees, and many companies do not have that infrastructure.

Socially, one of the biggest barriers is the belief that raising children and running a household is a woman's job. The man does not share these responsibilities. This leaves women with the double burden of trying to balance a professional career with domestic responsibilities, an issue that Arab women share with professional women in many other cultures.

> **Leading by example**
> Khadija bint Khuwaylid, who was Prophet Mohammad's first wife, was a very wealthy and successful merchant.

Huda Al Ghoson,[10] the most senior female executive at the oil giant Saudi Aramco, recalls the struggle she faced as a woman when she first joined the workforce in the early 1990s: 'When I was Aramco's supervisor of housing policy, a Saudi male asked to transfer out of my unit. He told my supervisor that if his family knew that his boss was a woman, it would ridicule his masculinity, and maybe he would be asked to divorce his wife. When my supervisor told me this, I said, "Absolutely, let the guy move out. I don't want to be responsible for a divorce." In addition, at one point I supervised an expat American woman. She said that, number one, she would not work for another woman and, number two, she would not work for a *local* woman; she thought the expatriates had come here to

---

10   Quotes are taken from an interview with Huda Al Ghoson, published in the *McKinsey Quarterly*, February 2015.

teach us, not to be managed by us.[11] I told her I wouldn't force anybody to work for me but asked her to stay in my unit for three more months. She did and then withdrew her request to transfer out.'

Do not forget that you are dealing with people, not cultures and each individual is different. And don't forget that the degree of social conservatism differs from country to country – the Gulf countries are more strict and conservative than Iraq, Jordan, Palestine and Egypt, while Lebanon, socially, is the least conservative of all.

The most important rule you must keep in mind when interacting with Arab women in the workplace is do not be deceived by her external appearance. Whether she is dressed in fashionable Western-style clothes or wearing the traditional Islamic hijab[12], it is always better to behave and interact with her in a reserved and conservative manner. Do not assume that just because she is in a senior position and wearing a designer business skirt-suit that she thinks and behaves like an American businesswoman. The rules of her society still apply and determine what is appropriate behaviour and what is not.

> **Yemeni Nobel Prize-winner**
>
> Tawakkol Abdel-Salam Karman won the Nobel Peace Prize in 2011. She is a Yemeni journalist, politician and senior member of the Al-Islah political party, and human rights activist. She leads the group Women Journalists Without Chains, which she co-founded in 2005.

---

11   See also 'The condescending attitude', page 103.

12   See 'Appearance and dress codes', page 156.

So if you have a business engagement with an Arab woman and you are not quite sure if it would be appropriate to meet over a lunch or coffee in a restaurant or hotel lobby, take your cue from her, follow her lead; she will decide what is appropriate for her.

Tari Lang, a communications and leadership adviser who has been working in Jordan, the UAE and Oman for over ten years, says: 'I did not feel that my being a woman mattered. I never felt I was treated less respectfully because I was a woman.' Jonghee Son, who works in the travel and tourism sector, says she actually found it easier being a woman in Jordan. 'When they see me, a woman from the Orient, and I am small, they instantly want to help me. They are very kind. So being a woman was an advantage here. But you have to be very careful how you behave and how you dress because you will lose respect. You have to be aware of the social taboos here and you must behave properly. Then you gain trust and respect. It all depends on what you do.'

Mothers and the Prophet

When a woman becomes a mother, she achieves a somewhat elevated status in the Islamic culture and her needs and demands become the first priority of her children.

It was narrated by Abu Hurairah that a man came to the Prophet (pbuh[13]) and asked him who amongst his near ones had the greatest right over him. The Prophet replied, 'Your mother.' The man then asked, 'Who after that?' to which the Prophet replied again,

---

13   Peace be upon him. A phrase used when mentioning the name of the Prophet.

'Your mother.' Asked who is next, the Prophet again replied, 'Your mother.' When the man asked who after that, the Prophet said, 'Your father.'

In another narration the Prophet Mohammed (pbuh) said, 'Paradise lies at the feet of mothers.'

THERE IS NO HONOUR IN CRIME

So-called 'honour crimes' are the most notorious forms of violence against women in many cultures where 'honour' is held as a central value. The common belief in these societies is that the men are the active generators and guardians of that honour, while the only effect that women can have on honour is to destroy it.

Human Rights Watch defines 'honour killings' as an act of vengeance, usually death, committed by male family members against female family members, who are believed to have brought dishonour upon the family.

The honour-based system is unforgiving: women who are suspected of dishonouring their families are not given an opportunity to defend themselves, and the male family members have no socially acceptable alternative but to remove the stain on their honour by attacking the woman.

The use of honour and shame as justifications for violence and killing is not unique to any one culture or religion. Honour killings have historical roots in many regions of the world, including Latin America, Europe, the Middle East and South Asia, and are reflected in many works of literature worldwide.

While in most cases honour killings are not religiously motivated, they have been recorded across Christian, Jewish, Sikh,
Hindu and Muslim communities. There is no mention of honour killing in the Quran or Hadith (the Hadith describes the
teachings and actions of the Prophet Mohammed). Honour
killing, in Islamic definitions, refers specifically to extra-le-
gal punishment by the family against a woman, and is forbidden by the Sharia (Islamic law).
Religious authorities disagree
with extra punishments such as
honour killing and prohibit it, so
the practice of it is a cultural and
not a religious issue. However,
some do use Islam to justify honour killing, even though there is
no support for it in Islam.[14]

> **Queen Rania**
> Queen Rania, the wife
> of King Abdullah ll of
> Jordan, is a strong advo-
> cate of women's rights
> issues and a leading sup-
> porter of changes in hon-
> our-killing legislation.

While the use of honour as a cultural justification for killing
is in line with the mindset of certain groups, it's not possible
to generalise about an entire population, as many people from
the same country would not share that belief system.

---

14 Report by the Canadian Department of Justice, Preliminary Examination of so-called
'Honour Killings' in Canada, 2013.

3

VALUES, BELIEFS AND VIEWPOINTS

HONOUR, RESPECT AND REPUTATION

The central importance of honour, dignity and pride to the Arab mentality cannot be overestimated. The core drivers for behaviour in Arab culture are to safeguard and enhance a person's honour and avoid shame. And since the person does not only represent himself but also his entire family and tribe, the belief is that any dishonourable behaviour would reflect not only on the individual, but also on his entire family. And since the community and society are the judges of what is considered honourable and acceptable behaviour, it is therefore not surprising that Arabs put such a big weight on reputation, public perceptions and what people think and say.

'One theme that comes up time and again is dignity,' British Ambassador Peter Millett notes. 'Dignity in the Arab world is hugely important – perhaps more important to Arabs than it is to people in the West. Dignity is that people respect you and recognise that you are someone, not necessarily important, but that you are a person who deserves respect.'

'In Japan, modesty is very important in our culture,' Toshihiro Abe says, reflecting on some of the differences he has experienced. 'We are taught that we should not talk about ourselves in front of people, and that we should be very modest. But here pride is very important and we have to be very careful how we speak so as not to hurt the other person's pride.'

It took Tony Goldner, a consultant from Australia, some time to realise the role that honour plays in this part of the world and how it drives people's behaviour, what they say and what they are willing to do. 'That has affected the way I do my work by having to think in a different dimension; trying to be empathetic and trying to put myself in their shoes and imagine what trade-off they are trying to make. Particularly in some of the places I have advised and worked with senior officials in government, that's an extra over layer on top of everything else that they have to be worried about, and it's hard. I have had to develop this ability, because especially in the early stages of the relationship, the client is still not willing to be open and candid and say I cannot do this because of this person or that issue. It takes a while to get to that place where they bring you into their thought process, but once you are there, it is amazing to see.'

A DIFFERENT CONCEPT OF HONOUR

Patrick, a senior consultant in a UK-based firm, was talking to me about some of the difficulties he was facing working with a VIP client in one of the countries in the Gulf. He explained: 'There are some things I just cannot seem to get my head around. My firm was hired to do the PR work for this very influential client. We agreed that a series of articles, including an interview in one of the major newspapers in the UK, would be ideal. So I use my contacts to get the journalist – who is

extremely busy – to agree to fly out to the Gulf to do the interview. After several delays, we get a date fixed, only to get it
cancelled at the last minute.'

Patrick's confusion and frustration were very clear: 'I don't
understand. If honour is key in the Arab culture, how can
this person cancel at the last minute? Did he not tarnish his
honour when he did not keep his appointment and upset the
journalist?'

It is easy to see Patrick's dilemma. So I attempted to show
him the picture from a slightly different perspective. It did
not change the situation, nor did it make it right in his eyes,
nor does it mean that he must agree with the behaviour; it just
helped shed some light on the situation, ease his frustration
and helped him be better prepared to handle things in a different way in the future.

I reminded Patrick that the judge of whether a person's behaviour is honourable or shameful is not a foreigner but rather the
person's group and community, which are far more important than any other relationship. And since the person does not
only represent himself, but his group and the wider community, then something might have happened that changed the
situation on the ground. Patrick's Arab client therefore needed
to make sure that it was still okay for him to voice certain
opinions to a foreign journalist. And I am certain there was no
intention to insult either the journalist or Patrick.

My advice for Patrick was to invest in nurturing a closer
relationship with this senior person and also with the people
close to him, who provide him with support and advice and

can influence his decisions. These relationships would allow Patrick a clearer understanding of what is going on behind the scenes and would help him anticipate any shifts and changes.

SAVING FACE

The notion of 'saving face' is extremely important and must be understood by anyone wishing to build long-term success-ful relationships in the Middle East.

It is an especially critical point to keep in mind during nego-tiations. If your objective is to save the relationship and reach win-win solutions, then you must find a way to give your Arab opponent an honourable way out that would save his face in front of his people.[1]

Tari Lang learned that lesson after having gone through an experience that ended up costing her a business contract. 'There was one incident of conflict I had with a client which started because we had not set out the ground rules clearly from the start. As the conflict escalated and I wasn't careful enough about allowing him a way out from losing face – and he was about to lose face in a fairly major way inside his organisation – things just got worse. I feel if I had given him a way out, we probably would have resolved it much more to both our satisfaction. But I failed to see that and as a result, he hardened his position. So now I have learned that if I see the potential for a conflict, I would stop and think, and I will think about it much more strategically, instead of how I reacted in that situation. That was a big learning point for me.'

---

1   See also 'Decisions, Risks and Contracts', page 120.

It is also essential to keep in mind the notion of saving face when giving any sort of feedback on performance. An Arab would generally find it difficult to separate his job performance from his person – i.e., as an Arab, what I do and who I am are one and the same. Therefore, any criticism of my performance can well be taken as direct criticism of my person and could be interpreted as shaming.

THE BLAME GAME

For those same reasons, an Arab would be very reluctant to admit a mistake or to make an apology. He would, however, know what he did wrong and would attempt to correct it one way or another, but an open confrontation, or blaming and shaming, would be very unwise.

Tari Lang had difficulty in handling this aspect of Arab culture. 'Because people did not want to lose face, they did not want to be the person seen to be doing anything wrong. So if anything went wrong, I know as an outsider I would probably take the blame.'

Jonghee Son, who works in travel and tourism, faces the same issue. 'Everybody can make a mistake, but what frustrates me here is that they are reluctant to admit the mistake and take responsibility. It is always "not me, not me". But I am not talking about you personally, I am talking about the company you represent.'

An Arab will not forget a person who handles a situation in such a manner that does not result in the loss of face by anyone. This can be quite difficult for a non-Arab to absorb, but rest assured that this will not go unnoticed. Stay calm, keep the conversation private, and choose your words carefully.

THE DOWNSIDE

Unfortunately, as is the case in every culture, there is a flip side to most values when they are taken to their extreme. Because so much focus is placed on avoiding shame and establishing honour, people may feel driven to establish honour at all costs. When the society is the judge, and safeguarding one's honour in the eyes of society is the main goal, then people can be driven to cover up what society would deem dishonourable. This can lead some to live double lives – doing certain things behind closed doors while maintaining an honourable public image that is acceptable to the demands of society.

If one starts hiding one's actions in order to maintain the public perception that one is honourable, then numerous issues would undoubtedly arise that could negatively affect business and society as a whole.

Felix Bernhard, a German working in Jordan, found he was having trouble with this aspect of Arab societies: 'The one thing that I have had difficulty adjusting to here is how much people are concerned with their public image and showing what they have or what they are capable of. I know, of course, this exists in my country, Germany, as well and in many other cultures, but I feel it may be stronger here because of the powerful need for acknowledgement from the family and society. In Europe we are a very individualistic society. I can, more or less, say I don't care if somebody is looking at me because I am taken as just an individual. But here it is different. A

person's behaviour will reflect on the family that he represents, and he will therefore always attempt to portray himself,
and by extension his family or the group he represents, in a
positive light.'

Government and paternalism

The paternalistic nature of Arab society also extends to the role
people expect their governments and rulers to play. The government is expected to provide for the people, yet there is very little
willingness to pay taxes, and the sense of civic values, collective
civic responsibility and citizenship is sadly very weak across the
Arab world. This is very evident in the issue with littering and
smoking in public buildings.

Tony Goldner, too, has trouble accepting another aspect, which
he sees as negative: 'There is a level of tolerance for double
standards or holding two competing values at the same time. I
get this sense in the Arab culture there's a higher tolerance for
things that are perhaps contradictory but can coexist at the same
time in day-to-day life. For example, a belief in the importance
of a meritocratic system in a company or in a government, and
yet a willingness to use personal networks to work around a
meritocratic system. So there's these two competing value systems that co-exist at the same time and for people from my cultural context it would be difficult to reconcile and would cause
people a lot of angst. And yet here, I think people are able to
live with that and not get too upset about it.'

RELATIONSHIPS AND TRUST
Like other honour-based cultures, the Arabs attach great value
to building and nurturing relationships. Business is built on
relationships. And Arabs do take business personally and

would, more often than not, put the relationship above any other consideration.

In other cultures, business is quite impersonal. It is said that two Americans can meet at an airport and start a business together as long as they have a good product and the figures add up.

David, who has been working in the region for over seven years, now understands the difference: 'In Britain, let's say I was the director of the Middle East, and then someone else takes over my position. On that day, I stop talking to every-body and I automatically hand over my contacts to the new guy, because it is about the role, not the person. Here, it doesn't work like that; it is about knowing people and building up that trust. So I cannot just hand over my contact list to the person who succeeds me.'

In the Arab world, people must get to know you first and build a personal relationship before they can do business. You have to go through a certain amount of ceremony to build up the respect and the trust. People need to first get a feel for you and what you are all about before business can be discussed.

'I have found that people here value me taking the time to get to know them, listen to them, take an interest in them, an inter-est in their life and their culture.' Eric, a Swedish consultant who has been working in the region for over five years agrees on the significance of relationships in the Arab world. 'It does take time to build enough rapport or acceptance with whoever you want to deal with here, but once you have taken that time and you pass a certain point, then all of a sudden you are a friend, and you are someone they can trust. And once you get to that point, you actually have very meaningful business relationships with them.'

Toshihiro Abe has also discovered the great value Arabs attach to the comfort they feel in an established relationship: 'We have some small customers who buy very little from us; I tell them that it would be better for them to move to another supplier that can handle these small accounts. But they never accept. They say, "We have experience with your company for thirty-five years; I know you; why do I have to go somewhere else?" Toshihiro realises, 'Sometimes I have to think about the business, but sometimes I have to understand and respect the relationship with the customer and maintain it – even if common sense says that we can cut that business easily.'

Dan Monaghan has come to understand this difference with his own British culture: 'Here, everything is about the people and the relationships – the person's good track history, his family, his values, how he interacts with others – these are the things that carry more weight here than the deal that is being offered. In Europe, any business would go with the best deal rather than because it was offered by a particular person.'

Dan found that this outlook also affected the recruitment and hiring process. 'If someone was to come to me and say, "I know this guy, I can personally vouch for him," that would be very much taken into consideration. In the UK it would not necessarily come into consideration. I might take the CV and take a look at this person, but it would not hold as much merit as it would here.'

Tari Lang, who has been working in the region since 2000, has discovered over the years the close connection between doing business and personal engagement in Arab culture. 'If you want to be happy working in the Arab world, you have to be comfortable with that blurring between work and friendship, and it has to be genuine. If you put barriers around you, you are going to be miserable. I know that now.' Tari echoes my advice to others who want to work in the Middle East: 'I think if people go to the Arab world because they think it's a good business opportunity, I can earn a lot of money, they might get much more frustrated and miss a wonderful opportunity of working with people who are just great people to work with. I found Arabs to be incredibly warm and friendly. I really think you have to put much more of your emotion into your work if you want to be successful but also enjoy it, because otherwise you will be angry a lot of the time.'

'I have found, very often that Western companies as a whole are not prepared to invest the time in the relationships,' ambassador Peter Millett observes. 'That is what's crucial for doing the business here. Not coming breezing in, thinking you can do a deal on one or two meetings. You have to invest time; you have got to come back quite a few times, build up that relationship, and then business will come your way if it is the right product and the right price.'

After over fifteen years in the region Tari now sees the true value of these relationships: 'What is interesting is that more than anywhere else in the world, I am still friends with people who are no longer my clients, people who didn't become my clients, though I wanted them to become my clients. In other words, it is not just work. I'm friendly with all of my ex-clients there, and if I didn't do business with them that would be fine, because they would still be friends. Yet in Europe, if you stop being a client, the chances are you would stop engaging with that person.'

THE COMMUNITY AND THE INDIVIDUAL

In Western culture, the focus is on the individual: each person has responsibilities and it is up to that person to get the job done. Efficiency and competition are values held in high esteem in countries such as the UK, Germany, the US and Australia. People are motivated by competitive situations as they strive to excel and stand out from the crowd. The hero in the US is the rugged lone cowboy, constantly on the move, single-handedly fighting the villain and conquering the Wild West.

On the other hand, like other honour-driven cultures, people in the Arab world place a higher value on the community as opposed to the individual. Hence people feel they do not only represent themselves but the entire community or group they belong to. According to the situation, that group or community could be the family or tribe, the organisation, or a group of people who share a specific background or status within an organisation.

The group becomes a support mechanism for the individual in both the good and difficult times. But the group also holds the individual accountable for his behaviour, ideas and decisions and determines whether a person's behaviour is honourable or shameful. Communal tribal traditions and values result in a natural tendency to form silos and territories – groups that an individual feels accountable to.

The result is that sharing one's ideas and opinions is no longer so simple and straightforward.[2] A person may feel pressured into stating an opinion or taking a position, however, this is not necessarily final, as it may need to change once the person has made sure that his opinion is in line with the opinion and interests of the group to whom he is held accountable. This becomes particularly relevant in a negotiation, where the person sitting at the table must repeatedly go back to his people to check that he has their support on every point and detail.

However, things are never quite so simple. Although the sense of community is strong, within that, there is a drive for the individual to take credit and stand out among his own group and peers. James Thomas, a corporate culture specialist who has been working in the region for over seven years, describes it accurately: 'The hierarchal nature of Arab societies and corporations creates a structure where you have the senior manager and a unit, and that forms a commune, so within that, a person gets protection from the fact that he has senior people above him whom he trusts will look after his group. Within that then, within the peer level, he wants to be the one that grabs the credit so that he can potentially move up to the next level. So yes, people want to fit within a structure that says yes this is where I belong, but against my peers, I need to be the one that grabs the credit to make sure that I am the one who moves up because there is a whole bunch of people competing for the same thing.'

---

2   See also 'What do you think?' page 60.

WHAT DO YOU THINK?

It is not easy for a person from an honour-based culture to be asked for his or her opinion. I do not only represent myself but also my group/my family/my tribe. And if my honour is linked to the group I represent, then I will undoubtedly have to be very careful that any opinions I express are in line with the stance and opinions of my group. Consequently, if for any reason I was pressured for my opinion – at the negotiation table for example, or at a brainstorming session – then I would have to say what I thought, knowing full well that I may have to change it once I have consulted with the rest of my group.

One way of avoiding such situations is to hold a series of smaller prep meetings, which would allow people to consult with their 'groups' beforehand, while also giving the chairperson a sense of the underlying issues before the actual wider discussion where decisions are expected to be made.

THE ASCRIBED STATUS

How does one achieve status in the Arab world? How are rewards distributed within an organisation? And how are people recognised?

While in the US, for example, a self-made person is greatly admired, in Arab culture, a person's accomplishments are important, but his family name, connections, relationships and even years of service account for a lot more weight in the 'being-based' or 'ascribed'[3] culture of the Middle East.

---

3   One of the 12 Dimensions of Culture used by KnowledgeWorkx to map cultural

Certain people may get extra privileges or breaks because of the tribe they belong to or the university degree they carry or the years of loyal service to the organisation.

> ### A degree of pride
> Arabs also take great pride in their university degrees, and parents work hard to see their sons graduate as doctors, engineers and lawyers.

Almost every non-Arab I have spoken to has found this aspect to be the most difficult to accept in Arab culture. Coming from a 'doing-based' or 'achieved' culture, where everything is about meritocracy, the individual's achievements and work, regardless of any other consideration, the ascribed culture, to Westerners especially, is very confusing and frustrating. Adding to the confusion is the fact that the ascribed status is rarely ever clearly stated, but rather implicitly understood and accepted.

The ascribed-status culture is neither right nor wrong; it is simply different. An achieved-status culture does work, and does deliver results too. A person who is ascribed a certain position will feel honour-bound to perform well in order to save face and prove to his people that he is deserving of the reward. And don't forget that Arabs strongly identify themselves with what they do.

Having said that, of course there is a downside. Things are different in government organisations or the large corporations that have spun out of quasi-government institutions,

---

motivators for behaviour. Marco Blankenburgh, *Inter-Cultural Intelligence: From Surviving to Thriving in the Global Space*, 2013.

such as oil and gas and telecoms. These large corporations are required to recruit and hire large numbers of nationals who are not necessarily qualified for their positions. Instead of subsidising these people with government grants, they are given jobs in these quasi-government corporations. The result is that you will find people in positions who are either incapable or unwilling to take the decisions required of that position; or they are simply disengaged and not interested in working – yet they get their monthly salaries and sometimes even a bonus and a promotion at the end of the year.

It is important for you to grasp this so that you are able to better understand the inner workings of any company or organisation as well as the underlying issues that influence decisions, especially when it comes to human resources, rewards and hiring policies.

Eric, a senior management consultant, agrees that governance practices, especially in large organisations, remain a major struggle in the region: 'You end up with some quite awkward structures in organisations in the eyes of someone from the West. This becomes much more of an issue for companies who are acquiring other companies outside of the region, which is putting more demands on companies here to introduce good governance practices and checks and balances.'

WHAT REALLY MATTERS
Against the backdrop of all these beliefs, values and viewpoints, and this seemingly contradictory setting, how then do you motivate staff in the Arab world?

Several surveys and studies have been conducted on the subject. The results of one such survey is in the box on this page. James Thomas agrees with the survey's findings: 'There is a shortage of credit-giving, so people are not saying thank you and well done enough, meaningfully in public recognising other people, such that everyone is comfortable that everyone is getting recognised for what they are doing. As a result, I have found that people are constantly seeking credit and recognition.'

Toshihiro Abe sensed this early on. 'I found that job titles are so important to Arabs, much more than they are to the Japanese and, I think, most other cultures. I think it might be related to the issue of pride.'

Motivating employees

A survey conducted in 2013 on employee motivation in the Middle East found that almost 75 per cent of respondents believe that a good work–life balance is the most important source of motivation after pay. This is followed by recognition of work and achievement (47 per cent), and training and development opportunities (45 per cent). However, 39 per cent claim they receive little to no support from their organisations to maintain a healthy work–life balance.[4]

In addition to the job title, such things as the size and location of the office, or even the size of the desk and the chair, and the number of vacation days are all extremely important symbols and forms of recognition. Travel assignments and training workshops are also very often used as means

---

4 Survey conducted by bayt.com and YouGov on Employee Motivation in the MENA region, January 2013. Survey covered: UAE, KSA, Kuwait, Oman, Qatar, Bahrain, Lebanon, Syria, Jordan, Egypt, Morocco, Algeria, Tunisia.

of distributing rewards evenly among staff. Management would make sure that everyone gets their turn, regardless of whether it is part of that person's personal development plan and job performance.

WORK–LIFE BALANCE

The importance and value of the job and work itself differs from culture to culture. Some live to work, and others work to live. While Americans boast about working sixty or seventy hours a week and are satisfied with only two weeks of vacation per year, in the Arab countries – similar to some Mediterranean cultures – less value is given to *work* and more to *living*. Employees get about two weeks of vacation on top of at least another fourteen days of public holidays.

The point here is that you should not expect your Arab co-workers (generally speaking) to keep the same weekly work hours as you do, or to be as willing as you are to sacrifice things for work. For an Arab, work is part of life, not life itself, and leisure time spent with family and friends, which carries great value, may not be readily sacrificed for a job. Especially in government departments and the military, where people are not compensated for any overtime work, you will find very little willingness to spend any time working past the official working hours of the day.

It took Alexis McGinness, an American working in the development aid sector, a while to understand this, but then she was able to help her newly appointed American boss: 'My new boss was calling for meetings at 4 p.m., although our official working hours finished at 4.30. He thought that people should stay longer. But I explained that here people come for work, but they have a second life, they have their family, they need to leave, they only put in their eight hours a day and they leave.'

Don't forget that each person is different, and just because people may share the same values, it does not mean that they will behave in the same way.

THE *WASTA*

Viewed by many as a corrupt practice, *wasta* is an Arabic word that literally translated means 'go between'. The commonly used term basically refers to 'who you know' – who could help expedite whatever you need done, or maybe even slightly bend the rules to get you out of a pickle. (It doesn't necessarily have to be someone in a very senior position; a junior clerk in a government department can also be a very useful *wasta*.)

Forms of the *wasta* are, of course, present in different parts of the world as well. Still, many believe it is extremely damaging for the Arab world as it undermines the need for meritocracy. While many governments and advocates of the rule of law and good governance are working hard to diminish the *wasta* culture in their countries, a lot of people still view it as a benign practice that is a natural outcome of the tribal, social and political structure of the Arab world.

AVOIDING CONFLICT

Avoiding conflict and maintaining social harmony are among the key motivators of behaviour in the Arab world. Seeking consensus is an important Arab and Muslim tradition.[5] Pushing a point or open confrontation – even though you are certain that you are right – will not get you anywhere. Eric puts it nicely: 'You cannot push a piece of spaghetti, you have to find ways to pull it.' So you need to understand the different dynamics at play. How do you achieve your objective in a way where others also see the benefits to them and their organisation and those around them?[6]

Tony Goldner experienced this first hand when his driver, who had worked with them for a couple of years and with whom they had a very good relationship, decided to quit his job. 'We went away for holiday for about a month and when we got back, our driver sent me a text message saying that he will no longer be working for us and wished us the best of luck. I emailed him and tried to call him several times, because I wanted to know if there was any problem or if there was something we could do to change his mind, but he just avoided the confrontation and did not respond. I eventually gave up. I understood later that he just wanted to avoid an awkward situation.'

FAITH AND FATE
People have different ways of looking at the world. A key difference is the concept of 'fate' – do we control circumstances or do circumstances control us? Is what happens a function of what one can do or is it down to forces outside of one's control such as fate, luck or who you know? Whatever your belief, it

---

5　See also 'A decision is made', page 120.

6　See also 'Bad news', page 100.

will undoubtedly affect the way you approach business, negotiations and life events in general.

In the West there is a strong belief, or perhaps it is just a perception, that individuals control their destiny and influence
the course of events. We predict the weather, set goals and
plan the future. 'If I work hard I will succeed.' 'I am the captain
of my ship.'

In the Middle East, however, the belief or perception is that we
have little control over circumstances or what happens; events
– whether good or bad – are controlled by external forces such
as fate and luck. This can lead to quite a few misunderstandings, especially when it comes to business planning. A businessman from North America may interpret this behaviour
as passive or even lazy, while an Arab would interpret the
behaviour of the North American as controlling, aggressive
and even pushy.[7]

While Western cultures are largely secular, in the Arab world,
religion and the state are very much intertwined. Islam is a
way of life and has a very strong influence over Arab culture,
especially in this area.

The word Islam in Arabic means the willing submission or
surrender to the will of God. It describes the state of mind of
anyone who recognises God's absolute authority, and reaches
a conviction that God alone possesses all power; no other
entity possesses any power or control independent of Him.
The concept of *qada'a wa qadar* – fate and God's will, the

7   See also 'Plans and planning', page 141.

belief that it is all in the hands of the Almighty, is central to the Islamic faith and therefore to the Arab outlook on life.

From an Arab's point of view, if things do not work out, then it was not meant to be: 'God willing it will work out the next time.' It does not mean that one should stop working, but there is a sense of total resignation to God's will. On the other hand, a West European or an American would want to establish what went wrong and who was responsible for it, analyse each and every element – after all, are we not in control of our destiny and are we not the creators of our own circumstances?

INSHALLAH

Inshallah literally means God willing. This is the one word that you will hear said more often than any other across the Arab world, regardless of a person's social status, education or background. *Inshallah* is said when someone intends to do something or wants something to happen.

God willing

In the early 1900s, the English often used the Latin phrase *Deo volente* – which also means 'God willing'. In conjunction with a signature at the end of letters, it was used to signify that 'God willing' this letter will get to you safely, or 'God willing' the contents of this letter come true. The term was then abbreviated and simply used as DV.

Although the word *inshallah* is linked in many people's minds to a negative perception, it is not necessarily so. Most foreigners' reaction when they hear the word *inshallah* is a bemused smile and the thought that whatever it is they have asked for is not going to happen. For Alexis it meant 'maybe;

eventually; or not'. But she also realised that it depends on the context and how the word *inshallah* is used and who uses it.

For many, the word is used to genuinely mean: All acts of God aside, I will get this done for you; I will do my best but I cannot tempt fate or be arrogant enough to think that it is all in my control. Still, however, there are people who use it as a way of getting out of a commitment.

Graham Ball, who has been working in Lebanon for well over a decade, says, 'When I take something into the shop for repair and I ask, "When will it be ready?" I get the response: "Three o'clock, *inshallah*." So I ask, "Does that mean it will be ready at three or not?" The response is always: "It means three o'clock, *inshallah*."' Graham laughs and goes back the following day at three o'clock without a lot of hope – sometimes he is justified and at other times he is pleasantly surprised that it is ready exactly on time.

Dan Monaghan found that he had trouble with the overuse of the word *inshallah*: 'For me, when I first came to Kuwait it meant basically, If I want to do it I'm going to do it. It was very much like … I'm going to drink my tea, I'm going to smoke my cigarette, I'm going to do whatever else I need to do before it happens.'

So when you hear the word *inshallah*, I would advise you against rushing to an assumption or conclusion; give the person the benefit of the doubt, but at the same time manage your expectations.[8]

---

8 See also 'Perception of deadlines', page 142.

THE EVIL EYE
People across the Middle East share a relatively strong belief in the evil and destructive power of envy – or what is also known as the evil eye – which the Holy Quran warns believers against. There are several practices that are common to avoid its negative effects, such as displaying the dark blue beads that resemble an eye alongside religious symbols and verses from the Holy Quran, as well as the burning of incense in special burners.

People may also refrain from speaking publicly about their success or their good fortune so as not to attract other people's envy and jealousy. And when things do not work out or something goes wrong, a large portion of Arabs are inclined to put that down to the supernatural power of the evil eye.

The importance of the individual
Don't forget, we don't deal with cultures, we deal with individuals. And each individual is different. Each person is the accumulated result of his own unique personal experiences and the influences of all the different cultures he has been exposed to through education, travel, interaction with different people, media and pop culture.

4

LIVING IN AN ISLAMIC COUNTRY

Although Islam is often associated with the Arab world, the fact is that only 20 per cent of Muslims are Arab and the majority (67 per cent of Muslims) live in the Asia–Pacific region.[1] Actually, there are more Muslims in the United Kingdom than in Lebanon, and more in China than in Syria.[2] Still, the Middle East and North Africa region has the highest concentration of Muslims living in one region – 93 per cent of its inhabitants are Muslim.[3]

Islam is a dynamic part of people's lives and governs personal, political, legal and economic aspects of their everyday actions and interactions. Toshihiro Abe found this to be significantly different from his own Japanese culture: 'In Japan we do not believe in religion, we are not a religious people. But here, religion is a strong part of everyday life and it is a source of discipline and respect for them. In Japan, discipline and respect are very important for us too and we learn them from our parents and grandparents at home but not through religion.'

---

1 Pew Research Centre, Factank article, 7 June 2013.

2 Pew Research Centre, Table: Muslim Population by Country, 27 January 2011

3 Pew Research Centre, Factank article, 7 June 2013.

The aim of this chapter is to provide you – as a foreigner living or doing business with this part of the world – with the basic information that will enable you to better understand how the Islamic religion affects Arab culture, traditions and way of life.

WHAT IT MEANS TO BE A MUSLIM

Islam means complete submission to the will of Allah (God)[4], and a Muslim is one who submits to Allah. A Muslim recognises the existence of the one and only true God; that God is eternal, transcendent and absolutely one; that God is incomparable, self-sustaining and neither begets nor was begotten. A Muslim recognises that Mohammed (pbuh) is the last prophet to bring revelation to mankind and that one day Allah will resurrect all human beings, and they will be questioned about their beliefs and actions.

The Muslim scripture is the Holy Quran. Muslims believe that the Quran is a record of the exact, unaltered words of Allah revealed through the Arch Angel Gabriel to Prophet Mohammed – who memorised and wrote down the words. The Holy Quran is therefore considered sacred and is treated with utmost respect and is usually placed on a special wooden stand to be read.

The Quran and the teachings and practices of Prophet Mohammed, as recorded in traditional accounts called Hadith, are the basis for all guidance in the religion.

---

4 Allah is the Arabic word for God and is used by both Muslims and Christians in the Arab world.

A person becomes a Muslim after publicly pronouncing the *Shahadah,* the declaration of faith (see below).

THE FIVE PILLARS OF ISLAM
These are the framework of the Muslim life, the five duties that every Muslim is obliged to perform. They are:

Al Shahadah:
The declaration of faith – 'I bear witness that there is no god, but God; I bear witness that Mohammed is the prophet of God.'

Alsalah:
Prayer – Muslims are required to pray five times a day.

Zakat:
Alms-giving – Muslims are required to give away a percentage of their earnings to those less fortunate, regardless of their religion.

Al Sawm:
Fasting during the month of Ramadan.

Hajj:
Pilgrimage to Mecca.

FIVE DAILY PRAYERS

Muslims are required to pray five times a day and each period for prayer has a special name. Prayer times are fixed by the sun and change daily. These essential times are:

1   After first light and before sunrise (*Fajr*).

2   Between the sun reaching its height and mid-afternoon (*Dhuhr*).

3   Between mid-afternoon and sunset (*Asr*).

4   After the sun has finished setting (*Maghrib*).

5   In the dark of the night (*Isha*).

Before approaching prayer, a Muslim must perform the *wudu* – a ritual washing that symbolises spiritual cleansing and purity in readiness for coming before God. It involves washing the hands, mouth, throat, nose, ears, arms up to the elbow and the feet.

Muslims worship in a *masjid* (mosque); however the daily prayers can be performed anywhere. Mosques very often have a domed roof and a tall tower called a minaret. Muslims are called to prayer from the minaret. The man who enters the minaret and calls them to prayer is called a *muezzin*.

There are no pictures or statues in a mosque. The interior is usually decorated with geometric shapes and Arabic calligraphy quoting words from the Holy Quran. Worshippers must remove their shoes before entering a mosque. The floor is covered with a carpet and there is almost no furniture because Muslims use prayer mats for prayer and many Muslims will carry their prayer rug with them wherever they go.

The prayer is always performed facing the *Qibla* – the direction of the *Kaaba*. Muslims believe that the *Kaaba* is the holiest place on earth. It is a cube-shaped building made from granite that is located in the centre of the great mosque of Mecca – the birthplace of the Prophet Mohammed (pbuh). The *Kaaba* is not worshipped but used only as a focal point for prayer, simply signifying a direction imposed by God to maintain unity and uniformity among worshippers. Every Muslim family, no matter where they live, knows what direction the *Kaaba* is from their house.

All public buildings and most offices will have a designated prayer room (musalah) – one for the women and a separate one for the men. There will also be facilities for carrying out the *wudu*. Worship can also be performed openly in public and takes priority over any other activity. However, actual observance varies from one Arab country to the other. In Saudi Arabia, everything will stop during prayer times – all the shops close and supermarkets shut down their checkout counters for the duration of the prayer time – which is about ten to fifteen minutes. In all other Arab countries, work continues as usual and individuals are left to decide for themselves whether they want to pray or not.

Friday is the Muslim holy day, when communal prayers are held at midday. Everything is closed on Friday and no work is done. However, some of the bigger shops and shopping malls now open after 2 p.m. on Fridays.

SUNNI AND SHIA

The vast majority of the world's Muslims practise Islam in its mainstream form, which is Sunni. Non-Sunni Muslims are known as Shia and they constitute about 10 per cent of the world's Muslim population. (Each of the two main sects have their own sub-sects.) The issue that originally separated the Shia from the Sunni Muslims is not a religious one but, rather, a political issue, namely the question of the succession of the Prophet Mohammed.

Sunni Muslims agree with the position taken by many of the Prophet's companions, that the new leader should be elected from among those capable of the job. This is what was done, and the Prophet Mohammed's close friend and advisor, Abu Bakr, became the first Caliph of the Islamic nation. The Shias believed that the succession

> **Shia Muslims**
> The largest Shia population in the Arab world is in Iraq. Sizeable numbers also live in Yemen, Syria, Saudi Arabia and Lebanon. Bahrain has a Shia majority, although it is ruled by a Sunni family.

should remain in the Prophet's family, and maintain that the Prophet Mohammed had designated his first cousin and son-in-law Ali to be his *khalifa* or successor.

ISLAMIC AND SHARIA LAW

Sharia is the Arabic word for Islamic law. The Quran is the first and main source of Islamic law, and lays down detailed rules that cover every aspect of daily life for Muslims. These rules render behaviours as either binding and obligatory, or forbidden, or recommended, or advisable. The second source of Islamic law is the Hadith, which is a compilation of the sayings and deeds as reported from the Prophet Mohammed. Islamic law and jurisprudence have developed out of the interpretation, elaboration and study of the Quran and Hadith.

The legal system

There is no single uniform Middle East or Arab law, nor is there one uniform legal system for all Arab countries. However, most of the Arab countries' legal systems are based on the Egyptian Civil Code, which was greatly influenced by the French Napoleonic civil code. Today all Arab countries except Saudi Arabia and Oman are civil law countries based fully or partly on the Egyptian Civil Code.

Understandably, there is a lot of fear and confusion among international business people regarding the nature of Islamic and Sharia law and its application to business. In all the Arab countries that have adopted civil codes and civil legal systems, Sharia plays a small role and is applied mainly in family matters such as marriage, divorce and inheritance.

Sharia law outside the Middle East

Most countries outside the Middle East do not recognise Sharia, although some countries in Europe, Asia and Africa have allowed their Muslim populations to use Sharia to govern divorce, inheritance and other personal affairs.

However, in Saudi Arabia, where there is no civil code, Sharia operates and applies directly as a common law of the country, both in commercial courts as well as in courts of personal matters. No other law is applicable if it's contrary to Sharia. For a businessman who concludes a contract with a Saudi company, or for a group of banks that provide syndicated loans to a Saudi client, it is indeed advisable to see whether the terms of their contract are valid or enforceable under Islamic law. Parties should take the prohibition of interest under Sharia into account when negotiating an agreement. Even excessive penalty clauses in a contract may be held unenforceable by the Saudi courts, based on the general principles of Sharia.[5]

Though Sharia is the common law of the country, Saudi Arabia has enacted a large number of items of legislation, the so-called 'Regulations', covering many fields of law including the Company Law, the Code of Commerce and the Tender Law.[6]

UNIQUE TO SAUDI ARABIA

The Committee for the Promotion of Virtue and the Prevention of Vice (abbreviated CPVPV), also informally referred to as Haia (the Arabic word for Commission) is the Saudi Arabian government's 'religious police' or Mutawa. Their role is to enforce Islamic values in accordance with the Sharia law within the country.

Members of the Haia ensure strict adherence to established codes of conduct, which they believe to be commanded by Islam. Offenders may be detained indefinitely; foreigners are not excluded. Unlike a regular, uniformed police force, the members of the CPVPV lack any law-enforcement training.

---

5 Article by Saleh Majid (Advocate (Iraq), and Faris Lenzen, LLM (London), attorney at law, *The International Construction Law Review*, volume 20, January 2003.

6 Article by Saleh Majid (Advocate (Iraq), and Faris Lenzen, LLM (London), attorney at law, *The International Construction Law Review*, volume 20, January 2003.

They dress in white robes and checked red-and-white head-scarves, and are known for their full beards; they are very much feared and disliked by the people in Saudi Arabia. They patrol the streets enforcing dress codes, strict separation of men and women, and making sure that shops are closed at prayer times and that Muslims perform their prayers. They also enforce the ban on the consumption and sale of alcoholic beverages and seize consumer goods and media that is regarded as being contrary to Islamic values and morals. In addition, they actively prevent any other religions from being practised within the country.

Members of the Haia or Mutawa have the power to shut down businesses and detain anyone who is seen to have broken any of their rules. Very few places are off limits for the Mutawa – among those are the offices of Saudi Aramco, King Abdullah University of Science and Technology, as well as all foreign embassies.

In 2007, King Abdullah bin Abdulaziz introduced reforms to regulate the Haia's powers – they were no longer allowed to carry the thin leather-covered sticks with which they beat alleged offenders and were barred from carrying out interrogations. Efforts by King Abdullah[7] to restrict their powers were met with a very strong push back from the conservative hardcore Wahabis.[8]

---

7 King Abdullah passed away on 23 January 2015. He was succeeded by King Salman bin Abdulaziz.

8 Wahhabisim is a branch of Islam that is described as ultra-conservative or puritanical. It is named after an eighteenth-century preacher and scholar, Muhammad ibn Abd al-Wahhab (1703–1792), who started the movement in Najd, a remote region in the Arabian Peninsula. Adherents often prefer to refer to themselves as Salafi – meaning 'following the forefathers of Islam'.

RAMADAN

Ramadan is the ninth month of the Islamic calendar, and a time when Muslims all over the world refrain from eating and drinking from dusk till dawn. The Muslim year is based on a lunar calendar, so Ramadan moves forward by ten or eleven days each year. The first day of Ramadan is determined by the sighting of the new moon.

Ramadan is a time of worship, contemplation and spiritual recharging. The Prophet (pbuh) said: 'If you do not refrain from bad language and bad actions, God has no need of your refraining from food or drink.' Ramadan is the month of charity and the time to strengthen family and community ties.

Every capable Muslim is expected to fast during daylight hours. During Ramadan, Muslims get up early before dawn and have a light meal. This time is known as *suhoor*. *Suhoor* is also the name given to the last meal eaten

> **Ramadan greetings**
> During Ramadan the traditional greeting *As salaamu alaykom* is replaced with *Ramadan kareem* – which means 'Ramadan is generous'. Or *Ramadan mubarak* – which means 'blessed Ramadan'.

before the fast begins. People tend to stay up very late during Ramadan and invitations to *suhoor* (basically a very late dinner served around midnight) are common.

At sunset (with the call to *Maghrib* prayers), families and friends gather to break their fast with a meal called *iftar*. Following the custom of Prophet Mohammed, the fast is often broken with dates, followed by a prayer and then a meal.

Non-Muslims are not required to fast; however, you must show respect and consideration and refrain from eating, drinking, smoking, or chewing gum in public areas, including offices. Such behaviour is considered illegal in many Arab countries, and could lead to fines and even time in jail.

Charity in the cities

It is common to see charity *iftar* tents set up in different locations in Arab capitals and cities. These tents are set up either by social or religious charity organisations, big businesses or wealthy individuals. They serve the *iftar* meal for anyone who walks in.

Ramadan has its own pace and social traditions that vary slightly from one Arab country to the other. In general, things slow down and the working day is made shorter to help ease the burden of the fast. Many businesses operate on a reduced schedule and shops may open and close at unusual times. In contrast to the slow pace during the day, Ramadan nights are bustling and alive with activities that continue very late into the night.

Night of Destiny

Layla al Qadr – known in English as the Night of Destiny, or the Night of Power – is believed by Muslims to be the night when the first verses of the Quran were revealed to Prophet Mohammed (pbuh); Laylat al Qadr occurs during the last ten days of Ramadan when Muslims believe the heavens open and angels come down to earth to determine the destiny of all people. People offer extra prayers during that night – many devout Muslims devote the last ten nights of Ramadan to continuous prayer in the mosque.

If you are invited to an *iftar*, make sure that you arrive about ten minutes before the call to the *Maghrib* prayer. Arriving too early will just stress your host – but make sure that you are not late, as the meal is served exactly on time. After the meal, people may sit around for some dessert and a cup of tea but will want to go rest for a little while before the evening activities commence.

Ramadan is considered the most important time of the year for all television stations across the Arab world. A wide variety of prime-time programming is created every year especially for Ramadan – from light-hearted game shows to soaps, and comedies to religious talk shows and epic dramas. Viewers across the Arab world follow these programmes, which often become topics of discussion and debate at gatherings and on social media.

THE *HAJJ*

The annual pilgrimage that must be undertaken by all Muslims is called the *Hajj*. It is the fifth pillar of Islam and a duty for all Muslims who are able both physically and financially to make the pilgrimage at least once in their lifetime. It is the time when Muslims of every ethnic group, colour, social status, and culture gather together in Mecca and stand before the *Kaaba* praising God together. It is a ritual that bonds Muslims together, showing that everyone is equal in the eyes of Allah.

Hajj is performed during a five-day period from the ninth to the thirteenth of *Dhu Al-Hijjah*, the twelfth month of the Muslim lunar calendar. *Umrah*, the lesser pilgrimage, can be undertaken at any time of the year. The pilgrims wear a simple white cloth called *ihram* and perform several acts of worship – among which is walking around the *Kaaba* seven times and then touching and kissing the black stone.

> ### The *Kaaba*
> The *Kaaba* – believed by Muslims to be the holiest place on earth – is a cube-shaped building made from granite and draped with a black cloth covered with verses from the Holy Quran that are embroidered in gold and silver thread. The *Kaaba* is located in the centre of the great mosque of Mecca – the birthplace of the Prophet Mohammed. When praying, Muslims must face towards Mecca.
>
> Non-Muslims are not allowed to enter Mecca.

RELIGIOUS HOLIDAYS

Eid is the time when the extended family get together and celebrate over big meals; children receive gifts from their parents and grandparents in the form of money – which they often use to buy chocolate and sweets – and close friends visit each others' homes to wish each other Eid Mubarak. Arabic coffee[9] is served along with dates and, sometimes, Arabic sweets.

These are the most important religious holidays in the Islamic calendar; however, not all of these are public holidays – Eid el Fitr and Eid el Adha are the only ones that are celebrated with a public holiday across the Arab world.

*   **Eid el Fitr**. Literally translated, this means 'festival of the feast'. This marks the end of Ramadan, the month of fasting. It lasts three days and it is a time for family and friends to get together, for celebrating with good food and presents for children, and giving to charity.

---

9   See 'Coffee and tea', page 174.

• **Eid el Adha.** The 'festival of sacrifice', which occurs seventy days after Eid el Fitr, is the second most important festival in the Muslim calendar. It is to remember the time when Abraham was going to sacrifice his own son to prove obedience to God, and marks the end of the *Hajj*. Sheep are sacrificed in memory of Abraham's submission to God and his willingness to sacrifice his son. This holiday lasts four days.

Eid greetings

It is customary for people to exchange greetings during Eid. The correct greeting is *Eid mubarak*, which means blessed celebration. It is acceptable to send *Eid mubarak* greetings in a text message; however, depending on how close your relationship is, it would also be considered very polite to convey your greeting in a telephone call.

• **Al Isra' wal Miraj**. Observed on the twenty-seventh day of the month of the seventh month in the Islamic calendar, this event marks the night that God took Mohammed on a journey from Mecca to Jerusalem and then to heaven.

• **Al mawlid al Nabaw**i. This is the Prophet's birthday. Sunni Muslims observe the Prophet Mohammed's birthday on the twelfth day of the Islamic month of *Rabi' al-awwal*, while Shia Muslims mark it on the seventeenth of this month. This is not usually a public holiday but is marked with speeches and prayers. Some Muslims view the celebration of birthdays as contradictory to Islamic law.

- **Ras alsaneh al hijriah**: The Islamic New Year is on the first day of *Muharram*, the first month in the lunar Islamic calendar. It marks the time when the Prophet Mohammed migrated from Mecca to Medina.

- **Ashura**: is on the tenth day of *Muharam* in the Islamic calendar. It is commemorated by Shia Muslims as a day of mourning for the martyrdom of Husayn ibn Ali – the grandson of the Prophet – at the battle of Karbalaa in Iraq. Many Shia will flagellate themselves in processions to the point of drawing blood in order to revere the martyrdom of Husayn, when he and some seventy companions were killed.

ARAB CHRISTIANS

Islam is the official religion in all the Arab states with the exception of Lebanon[10], officially a secular state. Arab Christians are indigenous to the region and many are descendants of pre-Islamic Christian Arabian tribes. Today, Arab Christians are well integrated in the societies they live in. In the Levant in particular, although in a small minority, Christians are represented in parliament, hold senior government portfolios, ambassadorial appointments as well as positions of high military rank.

According to the Oeuvre d'Orient Catholic association, there are an estimated ten to thirteen million Christians in the

---

10 Under the terms of an agreement known as the National Pact between the various political and religious leaders of Lebanon, the president of the country must be a Maronite, the Prime Minister must be a Sunni, and the Speaker of Parliament must be a Shia Muslim.

region. They represent 36 per cent of Lebanon's population, 10 per cent of Egypt's, 5 per cent of Syria's, 3 per cent of Jordan's and Palestine's, and 2 per cent of Iraq's population. Islam views the followers of Christianity as the 'people of the book', and therefore they are given protection and allowed to worship.

Arab Christians celebrate Christmas and Easter openly, with church services and celebrations in their homes. Christmas trees and decorations light up the shopping malls in Jordan, Egypt, Palestine, Syria, Lebanon and Iraq, where Christmas Day is a public holiday. Christmas is observed – meaning Christians can take the day off – in Oman, the UAE, Qatar, Kuwait and Morocco. Easter, on the other hand, is not a public holiday in any of the Arab countries except for Lebanon, which also observes several other saints' days.

Branches of Christianity in the Arab world

The majority of Arab Christians are Greek Orthodox, Latin, Roman Catholic, Melkite, Maronite in Lebanon, Copt in Egypt, Assyrian in Iraq (also known as Chaldean Catholics and Chaldo-Assyrians). Some Arab Christians observe Christmas according to the Eastern Orthodox calendar on 7 January, and some follow the Western calendar and celebrate on 25 December. The same applies to Palm Sunday and Easter.

RELIGIOUS TOLERANCE

Across the Arab world – including all the Gulf countries – non-Arab Christians are free to practise their religion in the many dedicated and licensed buildings, churches or in private homes. In the UAE, several churches were built on land donated by the ruling families of the Emirates in which they are located. And Kuwait's largest cathedral is located in the eastern part of Kuwait city.

Saudi Arabia remains the exception – and although there are a lot of expat Christians living and working in the Kingdom, there are no churches and any public display of the religion is illegal.

In most of the Arab countries – in particular the conservative Arab Gulf countries – evangelism and converting from Islam to Christianity is considered apostasy and comes with severe punishment by law.

Due to the large population of Indians in the UAE, there are three Hindu temples operating in rented commercial buildings in Dubai, one of which is used by Sikhs as well. Sikhs and Hindus living in Abu Dhabi and other Gulf countries also practise their religion in private homes.

A small Arab Jewish minority lived in Egypt, Iraq, Lebanon, Yemen and Morocco up until the establishment of the state of Israel in 1948, after which they immigrated to different parts of the world.

COMMUNICATION STYLES

DIRECTNESS AND SAVING FACE

If we go back to how important and central the concept of honour, pride and saving face is to Arab culture, then it is no surprise that Arabs in general value the indirect style of communication, which also allows them to avoid confrontation and conflict – another key motivator for behaviour across the Arab world.

Here, the priority or objective is not about 'saying what I mean and meaning what I say', but rather about safeguarding the honour of the other person and maintaining harmony while the message is being delivered. This is done in several ways, sometimes using a third party that may have influence on the people involved or by using parables, similar examples or stories from which the person can reach the proper conclusion and message.

While Chen Yi Xuan found this style of communication very similar to her Chinese culture, Giovanna Negretti found it difficult to understand at first. 'People go around and tell other people to tell you things. So let's say Khaled really wants to tell me something sensitive; he would tell Lisa, who would then tell Jalal, who would then tell me. For a long time I got very offended by this behaviour, but then I learned that it was really all about conflict avoidance[1] and the importance of saving face.'

For someone from a culture that values direct communications, this can appear to be time-consuming and frustrating because either some things are left unsaid or other things are not 100 per cent clear. However, for the majority of Arabs a direct style of communicating is considered aggressive, offensive and even rude, and could be interpreted as showing that the person does not care and is not interested in building a long-term relationship.

James Thomas, a corporate culture specialist working in the Gulf region, learned this the hard way. 'We were hired by a company that was having some problems with some of its business units. After doing the maths and all the logical analysis of the information we collected, we had our recommendations. So we stood up in front of the senior management team and said here is the answer. And we got slaughtered. By any objective measure, that was the right answer, and the CEO knew it was the right answer, but the way we did it – just going through the door, grabbing the data, going away and crunching the numbers and coming back with the answer – created this conflict.'

James later realised the value of understanding the alternative ways of communicating messages in this part of the world. 'Now I've learned that when I am trying to position those difficult messages, I make sure to invest the time to go and

---

1   See 'Avoiding conflict', page 65.

see the people concerned; we build it up slowly, so before we walk into the room, everybody knows there's no surprises. In a Western context, on page two you would have somebody tapping their finger saying, "Come on, get to the point." Whereas here you have to build up to the logic that got you to that point, so that by the time you get there, everyone is kind of, "Yeah, that makes sense," and nobody feels like they got a slap along the way. It is a much softer way of doing it.'

Toshihiro Abe found difficulty in getting people to open up and to speak their mind or say how they felt: 'My Japanese culture is reserved, too, in that way, but once people here feel they trust you and they open up, it is really wonderful.'

Coming from the Australian culture, which encourages people to be very direct and candid about what they think, Tony Goldner found he had to make a major adjustment in the way he communicated with Arab colleagues, clients and friends. 'Maybe it has something to do with the environment as well – Australia is a quiet, safe place to grow up and so there are really a few repercussions from being candid and direct and open, whereas here, life for a lot of people was much more complicated; family networks are much bigger, so it is likely that the economic and social consequences of speaking your mind are more dramatic in this context.'

The conflict-avoidance[2] nature of Arab culture also has a direct influence on the way people communicate their thoughts and how they approach problem-solving. This was another big learning experience for Tony: 'I had to moderate

2 See also 'Avoiding conflict', page 65.

my own communication style and my own way of expressing my thoughts so that I get the outcomes that I want and not end up running into a brick wall, or find that issues were unresolved because someone was being too polite to tell me that I was being too direct.'

Alexis McGinness learned that it is often about how a word or phrase comes out in English and the negative connotations it may have in the Arabic language. 'I have found that applies to emails as well. So I have had to adjust my way to include an opening sentence of courtesy before going into the subject.'

Jonghee Son, too, learned that she had to be careful with the words she uses: 'I found Arabs very emotional; they think emotionally, so you have to be really careful not to hurt their feelings. If you don't hurt them, you get everything, but if you hurt them or offend them, you will get nothing.'

As stated throughout, it is essential to keep the importance of 'saving face' in mind in all forms of communication – especially during meetings and negotiations. Never force a direct confrontation or raise your voice to an Arab, and never point a finger or demand an immediate decision or answer, especially in the presence of others. You will not get what you want and you will most likely end up losing the business.

Experience taught Tari Lang that a lot more listening and extra care were more important in the Arab world than in most other cultures. 'I now have learned how to be assertive in the Arab world without appearing to be disrespectful or insulting. What I would do differently is to ask more questions about the process and to ask for guidance from the people around the senior person I am working with. I would ask how would he or she normally do this, so I don't make mistakes in front of the person who is most senior and therefore least likely prepared to lose face. Because this is the person you have to protect.'

The importance of tone

The same principle applies to emails and telephone conversations. You need to pay extra attention to the tone of your email, because while your priority might be speed and efficiency, your Arab counterpart's priority will be getting the message across, but more importantly, maintaining respect, saving face and honouring the relationship.

DIRECT TALK

Still, there are aspects of Arab culture that are much more direct than in the West. For example, instructing people over whom one has authority is much more direct in Arab culture than in most Western cultures. And asking for a favour from someone in authority is considered normal and acceptable. It is also common for people to shout to express their displeasure or anger with someone, especially those of a lesser rank or status. This is similar to southern Mediterranean culture, where people let off steam and once they have done that, they go back to normal interactions.

David observed this while he was living in the region. 'In the street, people will get into an argument and very publicly shout at each other in a way that is a huge threshold to cross in most Western European cultures and from which you would never cross back into normal interaction. Whereas I found that Arabs are moving up and down that range much more easily.'

Arabs have a sense of inquisitiveness and curiosity and a genuine interest in getting to know others, which could result in some very direct questions that are considered normal in an Arab setting, but could cause offence to other more reserved Western cultures. Dan Monaghan found it strange that whenever he met someone in a social setting, the first question he was asked was, 'What do you do?' followed by, 'Where did you study and where do you live?' 'I found those questions intrusive, until someone explained to me that due to the nature of the Arab social structure and the importance of relationships, they were just trying to figure out where I fitted into certain circles. Here everything is connected, so they might know somebody in my line of business who may want to meet me, or they have a friend who may have gone to the same school I went to. So I learned that they were just looking for connections.'

When he was living in Jordan, David found that every time he got into a taxi he would have almost the same conversation, which would go something like this:

'Where are you from?'

'I am from Britain.'

'Ah, Britain – Manchester United. Are you married?'

'Yes, I am married.'

'Ah, very good. Have you got children?'

'No, I don't have children.'

'Oh. How long have you been married?'

'Eight years.'

'Eight years!! Have you been to the doctor??'

'Yes, but *kul shay fee yadday Allah.*' (Everything is in the hands of God.)

'Yes, yes, *subhan Allah. Hamdulillah.*' (Praise and thanks be to God).

This kind of questioning would be horrifying for the majority of people from the West; however, David didn't mind these conversations, because he knew that he could end it just by saying that it is all in the hands of God or that it is the will of the Almighty.

FACE TO FACE

While it is quite acceptable to pick up the phone and just get down to business in many countries, it doesn't work so well in the Arab world. Arabs prefer face-to-face meetings and conversations. People here must get to know you first and build a personal relationship before they can do business.

Toshihiro Abe believes this is one of the important things he had to adjust to in order to be able to successfully do business in this part of the world: 'Just sending an email doesn't work here. You have to see each other, talk to each other. It takes time.'

You have to go through a certain amount of ceremony to build up the relationship, the respect and the trust before getting down to business. They will want to see you, ask you about yourself and your family, and then eventually you do business. This is time invested that will go a very long way. So do take a little bit of time to

> **The personal touch**
> The need for face-to-face interaction might explain why, in spite of internet banking for example, many people still prefer to go into the bank or shop in person to get answers to questions or to resolve any issue that requires customer service.

talk about other 'safe topics of conversation'[3] before getting to the point of business. And you will need several face-to-face meetings before you can do business over the phone or via email.

When he first came to Dubai, Dan Monaghan would often send his deputy to meetings with a couple of the local companies they were starting to do business with. 'I started to sense that something was wrong; the deals were not going through and the local business owner who was attending the meeting was not happy because I was not there in person – even though they would get the same information, the same outcome as if I was there. But the fact that I didn't attend did jeopardise the relationship going forward. After that I realised the cultural importance of meeting the top person and the message that sent to my potential clients. I made sure that I maintained the contact face to face, and it has really paid off.'

---

3   See 'Topics of conversation', page 109.

Keep in mind that the younger Arab generation of professionals generally have a different approach to business meetings
that is more in line with international business practices, and
may therefore have much less interest in the social pleasantries and small talk; take your cue from your host.

PLEASING THE BOSS

Due to the hierarchal nature of Arab culture, people in
positions of authority, especially in the public sector and
the older more traditional generation, will try to assert their
power in ways that most Westerners no longer do. If an
Arab boss was very open, casual or behaved with too much
humility, he might be perceived as weak and not suitable
for his position.

Hence, the boss does most of the talking for his organisation,
company or department. Subordinates are there to corroborate
information or to provide technical advice and counsel to the
most senior person.

So if you are meeting with a senior government minister, you
will often find that there are several other members of his
staff also in the room, and therefore a lot of the boss's style of
communication – tone of voice, body language and choice of
words – will be for the benefit of his staff as much as for you.
There will be a certain amount of performing to save face and
assert his authority.

David realised that his Egyptian staff found his open, Western
style a bit confusing. 'I have learned that I, too, need to perform a little. So now when I am walking into a meeting with a

senior government minister, I do not carry my own papers and I ask my staff to do more things for me, so I act like the big guy and they take me more seriously.'

On the other hand, Chen Yi Xuan found she was having a much easier time with her Arab boss compared to her experience in her own country: 'In China, especially if you work for the government, you have to be very serious. The hierarchy is very clear. You must know your job and you must do it and you must show respect to your leader always. But here I can talk to my leader about a lot of things and it is very casual. In China it is not so casual.'

James Thomas has seen how some people fail to see the value of some of the things that the local culture ascribes importance to: 'For example, a management team comes in on top of a joint venture. Because it's a hierarchical culture, everybody is waiting for the big boss to tell them what the direction is, where are we going to go with this organisation. For the foreign manager, coming from a North American culture, his focus is: I will engage people when I have got a firm basis of what I want to talk to them about. But that does not work in this culture; people here just want to know who this person is, they want to meet him, they want to hear from him and they want to be heard.

'The months were going by and the organisation was getting more and more frustrated that this guy wasn't turning up, he wasn't telling them what the vision was. And they were starting to write off this new management team, who were probably going in the right direction, did have a vision for where they wanted to go, but they were just not

quite ready to share it. In the end they were alienating
the organisation because they failed to adjust their style
of communication.'

YES, NO, I DON'T KNOW

Getting a definitive yes or no answer can be a challenge in
the Arab world. One reason for that is the strong underlying belief that we are not in control of our destinies and that
everything is in the hands of the Almighty. The other reason is
the tendency to avoid giving bad news and avoiding the risk
of upsetting the other person, especially if it is someone in a
senior position or a foreign guest.

A typical polite response from an Arab client or official would
be, 'We are still looking into the matter and a decision has not
yet been made. We will be in touch.' Now this could mean
that the issue is still under consideration, or that the matter
is awaiting approval from a more senior person, or that they
are actually not interested in your product or service at this
time but are concerned about upsetting you, worried that a
rejection might affect any possible future transactions with
your company.

Tony Goldner has found this cultural aspect very different
from his own Australian, straightforward cultural style. 'As
a consultant trying to sell advisory services here, I often find
myself in situations where they say yes but they really mean
no or they mean not now, but they don't want to say no or not
now, so they say yes and then actually nothing ends up happening after that. One of the difficult things in the line of work
I do now is understanding when yes really means a yes and

let's move now to the next stage, or when yes means I am not quite convinced yet, so we may need to keep talking about it and that could take another six months. I am still learning how to tell the difference and it is hard to generalise; it depends on the personality of the individual and the context, but you eventually build a sixth sense in reading a situation and trying to understand what's actually going on.'

Keep in mind that the intention is not to tell a lie, but rather to keep things harmonious, knowing that somehow things will work out. In this case, the best thing to do is to be patient, occasionally following up without being pushy or demanding a final decision.

I would also advise to avoid asking questions that require a direct yes or no answer. So instead of asking, 'Will the report be ready on Thursday?' it is better to ask a question like, 'When do you think you can have the report ready?'

Giovanna Negretti still struggles with this aspect of the culture: 'I had a colleague who had a big pile of work; someone comes in to the office and says, "Can you do this for me?" And he answers: "Yes, sure." The person then walks out and I look at him and ask, "How are you going to do this?" And he says, "I'm not going to be able to but I cannot say no. If I say no, it's insulting." I know that it is not lack of honesty, but he just could not say no. It drives me crazy.'

For these same reasons, it would be wise for you, too, to avoid saying a direct 'no'; instead use language that keeps your chances open for future interactions and business.

In some countries in the Arab world, particularly in Egypt, when you ask a question, people are either embarrassed to say they don't know something, or they don't want to appear unhelpful by saying they don't know, so they will try their best to give you any answer. It's a running joke in Egypt that if you stop to ask for directions you may end up going on a wild goose chase because people will simply not say that they don't know.

BAD NEWS

Arabs will go to great lengths to avoid being the bearers of bad news, especially to their superiors. The result is that problems that could have been resolved at an early stage may be covered up or simply ignored. A bad truth is hidden until it either becomes apparent on its own or someone else brings it up. The tendency, when asked, is to keep saying that there is no problem and that everything is okay rather than go into detailed explanations of the problem and risk upsetting either someone senior or the foreign guest.

David, a senior diplomat based in Cairo, found that it was very difficult to get people who worked for him to say what was on their mind or to explain when they have a problem. 'So if I say to my driver: "You have been working very hard this month – do you need some time off?" he will never say, "Yeah, actually I am exhausted. I need the day off." And if I say to the staff, "I really want you to tell me if you have a problem in the office," no one will respond. However, they will respond if I ask them to tell me what could be better. But if I say, "Tell me if there is a problem. Do you have such and such a problem?" it tends to come second and third hand to me; people will not come to me and say, "I have a problem."'

James Thomas has faced the same issue in the Gulf: 'I have tried with organisations to have quarterly performance reviews where people have an opportunity to talk to a room of their peers and say: "You know what? I am struggling with this thing. What do you guys think about it?" It just doesn't work. Because people are not going to air that kind of thing in public. They want to say: "I am doing great, how about you?"'

And when a problem is addressed openly, the bad news is delivered in padded terms and in gradual doses. For example, it is not unheard of for a family member living abroad to be told that he needs to return home immediately because his mother has fallen ill when, in fact, she may have already passed away.

AGENDAS, MEETINGS AND PRESENTATIONS
Cultures have different cognitive styles or ways of thinking. Does the society focus on the forest or the trees? In North America and Europe the emphasis is on inductive thinking. People focus on facts and specifics, then use this information to draw general conclusions. But in the Arab world, the tendency is towards deductive thinking: people start with general principles then use these to analyse the details of the specific situation.

This can lead to some tricky situations. An American for example, will want to use details to build the framework of the partnership, while his Arab counterpart will first look at the framework, then move to the details. In the US, people tend to break down concepts and take a look at the parts. Thus, in a meeting, Americans will want a point-by-point agenda, while you will find that most Arabs, in contrast, are likely to prefer simultaneous discussions of all the issues, because they see that everything is somehow connected to everything else, nothing stands on its own, and every decision must be taken in relation to other issues and decisions. In communicating, Arabs focus on 'relationships' and connections between events, issues and objects and tend to speak using more verbs rather than nouns.

Again, this will differ with the younger Western-educated generation, who would more likely follow the international business practice of clearly defined meeting agendas.

Arab business people – especially in the GCC countries – have plenty of proposals presented to them on a daily basis. Therefore you need to grab their attention from the start by showing the immediate benefit to them locally. When giving a presentation for a business project or product, particularly in the initial phases, it is not recommended to use too much detailed data, numbers and charts if you wish to keep your Arab audience engaged.

Be prepared

If you are giving a presentation, make sure you are prepared in advance with the right technical equipment and electricity adaptors. The worst thing you can do is keep a senior executive waiting while you sort out a technical issue.

It would also be beneficial – especially if you are dealing with a public-sector entity – to prepare a short executive summary typed in Arabic that can be distributed at the end of your presentation. Make sure that the language and grammar is correct, otherwise your gesture would backfire and you would be seen as unprofessional.

THE CONDESCENDING ATTITUDE

The Arab world is a region that is going through unprec-
edented change at an incredibly fast pace – faster than the
experience of individuals in the region – which is why they
are very open to seeking advice and getting help from others.
But do not fall into the trap of assuming that you know better
because you are the 'foreign expert'. The awe that was felt by
the older generation of Arabs towards foreign experts is fast
eroding with the younger generation, who are educated in the
best universities and are just as knowledgeable as any foreign
expert. National pride is driving a trend across the GCC countries, in particular, to replace the large number of foreigners
with local nationals to manage their large corporations.

The most common mistake I see is Westerners coming in with
the patronising, even condescending attitude of 'we are the
experts, we know better, we are here to instruct you'.

Saif, an Arab executive in the defence industry, frequently
sees this kind of unhelpful attitude: 'These guys don't know
what they want, so just give them the most expensive items
and let's make the most money out of it. Or if it is a programme that is tight on funds, then just take this, this and that
out, although we all know that they will need these technical
specs for their operational requirements. The client's advanced
technical knowledge may be weaker. However, playing on the
client's weakness will only cause delays in the programme. It
is not a smart game to play.'

Eric also echoes Saif's observation: 'I have seen a lot of inci-
dences where Westerners have taken advantage of leaders and

situations here and have made themselves rich out of it. And the moment that happens, a feeling develops on the other side, and it is a big mistake; you won't come back. You just won't come back.'

The moment there is the sense an Arab is being taken advantage of, or they feel you have disrespected them by being carelessly arrogant or condescending, then you as an individual and as an organisation will have a problem conducting business here again. Arabs are very proud people. You need to be smart and find a way to pass on the required information in the form of advice, but never in the sense that you are instructing them on what to do or educating them.

Don't forget, these are very small communities, and everyone knows everyone; everyone is somehow related to or connected to everyone. So if you were in the respect zone, that moves around the network very quickly; the opposite is also true and it will cost you.

NEGOTIATING AND BARGAINING
Bargaining is very much ingrained in the Arab mentality and most Arabs would never shy away from an opportunity to bargain and negotiate a price down. Arabs in general are very price-conscious – regardless of how wealthy one is – and in the Gulf countries particularly, people are wary of being taken advantage of, especially by foreigners.

Therefore, always expect to be asked about your company's prices from the very first meeting. However, in order for you not to lock yourself into a figure that could negatively affect your chances for a business deal, it would be better for you to give a general, only indicative price at this stage. Until you have agreed to all the technical details and full requirements, it is best not to commit yourself to a price that you will not be able to later change. But be careful of first offering a very high price knowing that you will have to bring it down. Ending with a price that is significantly less than your initial offer will only raise your counterpart's suspicions and will most likely end up costing you the whole contract.

Once an interest has been expressed in whatever product or service your company is offering, then the bargaining and negotiating begins. Saif experiences this very often: 'There is no best and final offer in the Middle East. The client will always request changes. I have worked on cases where we went through seven best and final offers.'

Here, everything is on the table – other programmes or contracts, past contracts, other divisions that are part of the mother company – everything is connected; no issue or point stands on its own.

Expressing strong reactions and emotions is one of the tactics often used by the seasoned bargainer. You, on the other hand, should always remain courteous and calm and try your best not to show any frustration or anger. Be firm but always extremely respectful and never raise your voice to an Arab – especially not in the presence of others.

Be prepared for these negotiations to take a long time – depending on how large the contract is, it can take anywhere from one to three years to reach a final agreement. Flexibility is key. Be

> **Get authorisation**
>
> Make sure you have all the necessary approvals from your head office before engaging in the negotiations. Telling your senior Arab counterpart that the decision is not in your hands and that you will need to go back to your bosses for approval means that you have been wasting his time and that he has been talking to the wrong person.

prepared to keep amending your offer to demonstrate that you are listening to their concerns and working on meeting their needs. Introducing additional perks or services for the same price – such as free training for staff or maintenance work – is very helpful.[4]

Saif regularly faces these issues: 'A lot of our Arab clients ask for the final contract to be signed abroad; however, a lot of the Western companies I have worked with have strict regulations and refuse to cover travel costs. The company ends up losing a huge contract because of this lack of flexibility and lack of understanding of how to do business in this part of the world. If you want to succeed here, you must be flexible and proactive.'

Toshihiro Abe has found a certain level of passivity in some cases, and has realised the importance of consistently following up with his clients face to face: 'In Saudi Arabia, for example, we have a lot of customers who want to buy from us, but they will not initiate an order themselves; they wait for me to visit them and then they will give me their requirements.' But he found that slightly differs in other Arab countries. In Jordan and Lebanon for example, his customers would initiate an order without waiting for him to show up. 'However in

---

4   See 'Contracts', page 130.

Syria, they have a slightly different style; they wait for me to visit and then they start negotiating to get a better deal.'

BODY LANGUAGE AND GESTURES

Be aware of what you are saying without even speaking. Your body language, facial expressions and the way you carry yourself speaks volumes and will not go unnoticed in the Arab world. Do not slouch in your chair – this will be seen as a sign of disrespect. And I am sure you have heard this many times – do not sit with your ankle crossed over your knee; exposing the sole of your shoe in someone's face is considered a severe insult.

It is important to maintain eye contact, as this conveys trust, sincerity and honesty. But the point is not to stare the other person down. Keep it soft and natural. However, that rule changes if you are a man speaking to a woman or if you are speaking to an older man or someone very high ranking – prolonged direct eye contact is considered rude and challenging. When you are speaking to someone, try to face them with your whole body, not just by turning your head, and do lean forward slightly if you think what is being said is of importance.

Don't be alarmed by the stern, serious look that most Arab men wear on their faces – it's meant to be a sign of manliness but not unfriendliness.

SILENT OR LOUD

The meaning of silence, how it is used and the level of comfort people feel with it differs greatly from one culture to the other. Westerners find silence while in the company of others very uncomfortable and even embarrassing. Arabs, on the other hand, especially the older generation, are very comfortable sitting with friends and acquaintances in silence, simply enjoying the presence of the company they are with, or lost in their own thoughts, occasionally breaking the silence with a piece of news or some welcoming words.

While a popular Arab saying sees silence as 'a sign of consent and approval', it is not necessarily always so. Depending on the body language, silence could also be used as a sign of disapproval, or it can be used as a bargaining tool to get the salesperson to give a further discount on the offered price.

Silence is also seen as a sign of deep thinking and contemplation, particularly when talking to someone senior. However, be prepared for many interruptions, as Arabs fall within the polychronic[5] style of doing several things at once. So do not take offence and remain calm.

The volume at which the majority of Arabs speak – in general – can be considered too loud by most Westerners, who can sometimes mistake a normal conversation for an argument. 'When I first came here, when I heard people talking I thought they were fighting, and I thought it was because of me! I felt really uncomfortable.' Jonghee Son later realised that it was normal. 'Someone explained to me that maybe it is because a long time ago, when they were Bedouins, they were used to living in open spaces and they would shout across the space from one tent to the other.' Possibly. Maybe that could explain

---

5   See also 'Many things at once', page 140.

why the Japanese whisper, because they are used to living in their very small houses?

The higher volume in the Arab world is meant to reflect sincerity and enthusiasm. However you should try to keep your own volume in check, since it is easy to get the tone wrong and end up causing serious offence.

TOPICS OF CONVERSATION

'Don't talk about politics; don't talk about religion.' That is the advice Graham Ball received before coming out to the region. However, he quickly found that it is much more about being careful *who* you are talking to about politics and religion rather than avoiding those topics altogether. In most of the Arab world, and Lebanon in particular, you cannot have any kind of discussion without politics cropping up.

Nonetheless, before you delve into these sensitive topics you need to first educate yourself about the history of the region and its politics. Learn about Arab opinion on Palestine and the invasions of Gaza, Lebanon and Iraq, and the ongoing repercussions of the so-called Arab Spring. Be aware of the rivalries between the different Arab states before you suggest to an Arab official from a particular country to emulate a programme that you successfully implemented in another Arab country.

David, a diplomat who arrived in the region in 2007, was a bit anxious about engaging with people here. 'I thought they would have a hostile view of us because they hate the invasion of Iraq. But I found that in every place people in the Arab world are unbelievably generous, open and warm; even if they hate your country's policy, they love getting to know you as a human being.'

> ## Show cultural curiosity
>
> People in most Western cultures are quite indifferent to foreigners and show very little interest in them. In contrast, in the Arab world people treasure the opportunity of interacting with a foreigner and getting to know them. So when you show interest in their country, people really appreciate it.

Arabs are very hospitable and are quite willing to forgive foreigners their mistakes, as they expect them not to know a lot about Arab culture and traditions. An Arab would frequently try to explain political situations and how misrepresented and misunderstood they are in the Western media.

Nevertheless, because of the history of colonialism, as a foreigner, you need to be aware that you carry a lot of history with you that you have to account for. Peter Millett learned this the first time he was invited to a *mansaf*.[6] The host was a very young tribal sheikh whose father was also present. 'I remember sitting down and being quite businesslike in asking him about the Arab Spring. I could sense that they were not happy; they did not like that directness or that focus on their problems rather than our collective history. That was a lesson for me. I learned that talking about the historic relations is the right way to start.'[7]

---

6   The national Jordanian dish made of rice, lamb and a special yogurt.

7   See also 'Time and the past', page 146.

David also learned how to account for the history, which is not always pleasant: 'You have to account for it by displaying trust, displaying that you really care about and are interested in the country; that you want to learn the local language, you want to learn the expressions, you want to understand. So you need to invest a lot in the relationship. Be curious, be interested and ask questions, rather than having a point of view all the time.'

'It usually starts with, "I love America but I hate the president and your foreign policies."' Alexis says she is used to hearing these arguments but has never felt any hostility directed towards herself.

Like many other cultures, Arabs are willing to criticise themselves, but they don't want to hear foreigners criticising them. The history of colonialism makes this point even more significant. There's a very popular Arab saying: 'Me and my brother against my cousin; and me and my cousin against the stranger.'

Graham Ball has learned to handle this well: 'As a non-Arab, I would never criticise the Arab country I am in. And if somebody asks me, and says something like the situation in Lebanon is terrible, no electricity and water, my response is always the same, and that is: "I am a guest in your country, and you have made me feel very welcome. I stay in Lebanon, not so much because of the country, but because of the people."'

STORIES AND GOSSIP
Stories are very much a part of Arab culture and are used as an indirect means of communicating a message or teaching a

Telling tales

Al hakawati is the Arabic word for 'storyteller'. The Lebanese novelist Rabih Alameddine explains it in his epic novel that carries the same title: 'A *hakawati* is a teller of tales, myths, and fables (*hekayât*). A storyteller, an entertainer. A troubadour of sorts, someone who earns his keep by beguiling an audience with yarns.' Like the word *hekayeh* (story, fable, news), *hakawati* is derived from the Arabic word *haki*, which means 'talk' or 'conversation'.

lesson. In the old days, after the evening prayers, the men would gather in the tribal leader's tent or the ruler's palace and would share stories from the past. Sitting around an open fire, telling tales while sipping on the bitter Arabic coffee was the best way to pass an evening in the desert. You may recall the fictional Scheherazade of *One Thousand and One Nights*, who saved herself from execution by telling tales.

Those who excelled at storytelling became entertainers, educators and historians for the community. Through storytellers history was handed down from one generation to the other.

Arab culture is rooted in a strong oral rather than written tradition. Arabs enjoy sharing experiences and telling stories that are frequently infused with proverbs, idioms or a verse of poetry. So when your host starts telling a story, pay attention and don't switch off; there is a message in there for you, and as Vyasa[8] says: 'If you listen carefully, at the end you will be someone else.'

---

8 Maharshi Vyasa, also called Krishna Dvaipayana or Veda Vyasa, is a legendary Indian sage. He is considered the author of the ancient epic, the *Mahabharata*, the longest poem ever written. But he also plays a very important role in it.

Gossip – the negative version of storytelling – also became an enjoyment, with many societies in the Arab world thriving on it. Giovanna Negretti found this was similar to her Latino culture: 'The gossip is exactly like my culture. They love gossip here. Gossip, gossip about everybody. So I know things I know I shouldn't know about people's marriages, family problems and even their financial issues.'

CONSPIRACY THEORIES

Conspiracy theories are a prevalent feature of Arab culture and politics. Rarely is anything taken at face value in the Arab world. Intrigue and a conspiracy of some sort are believed to be behind every situation. This is not about ignorance or illiteracy; it is present among the educated and the highly qualified as well as the mainstream public. Suspicious of their official media, Arabs look to their family, friends and 'special sources' for 'the truth'.

But there is a background to it all. The belief in conspiracy theories is believed to have started when the Arabs were on the receiving end of a number of actual conspiracies: France and Britain did secretly conspire to carve up the Middle East between them with the Sykes–Picot Agreement of 1916. They also conspired to attack Egypt, with Israel's help, and thereby provoked the Suez Crisis of 1956. And more recently, it turned out there weren't any weapons of mass destruction in Iraq in 2003, despite what the politicians claimed.

While most of the conspiracy theories are quite bizarre and entertaining, some Arabs believe that the danger is in that they keep us from the truth and from confronting our faults and problems.

HUMOUR

Each of the Arab countries has its own distinct sense of humour coloured with its own local flavour. While Arabs do enjoy a good laugh at their own shortcomings, they are not particularly amused when they are the butt of someone else's joke – especially a foreigner's.

You need to be extra careful when using humour, as things will get lost in translation, and what might be funny in your own country may cause great offence in the Arab world. A light-hearted comment may touch on some sensitive local issues and have different innuendos in the Arabic language.

James Thomas cannot forget one of those embarrassing moments: 'I had one situation here where I made a throwaway comment without thinking about it, and the whole room just fell silent. We were playing an ice-breaking game where we had to use a bamboo cane. I got everyone to line up in two lines, and so they asked, "What are we doing here?" I was holding this cane and I said: "Oh, this is where the beating begins." For me it was completely a throwaway, light-hearted joke. But I could feel everyone instantly freeze. Fortunately, the person I said it to was a fiery individual and said something like, "I would like to see you try, you will come out of it worse." Then everyone laughed. But for those five seconds I just wanted the earth to swallow me. It was pure agony.'

LANGUAGE AND USEFUL WORDS

Arabic is the language spoken across the Arab world. However, there is a difference between written and spoken Arabic.

Written Arabic – also known as *Fus'ha* or classical Arabic – is the same across the Middle East. This is the language that is used in books, newspapers, television newscasts and official speeches. It is characterised by the use of repetition, heavy imagery and symbolism, and what Westerners may consider to be exaggeration. Spoken Arabic, however, differs from one country to the other – with each having its own local dialect and in many cases a different vocabulary.

For example, for an Egyptian *laban* means milk. But if he was to go to Jordan, Syria, Lebanon or Palestine and ask for *laban*, he would get yogurt. Similarly, a Jordanian who asked for *lymoon* in Lebanon would expect to get a lemon, but would get an orange instead.

All the Gulf countries have a very similar dialect, apart from Iraq, where the dialect is close, but has its own dialect and different meanings for some words. The Syrian dialect is very similar to the Lebanese, which has been made popular by very famous singers and musicians.[9] While the Jordanian dialect is very close to the Palestinian, Egypt is very different but is the most widely understood across the Arab world, thanks to the thriving film and entertainment industry in Cairo and the huge number of Egyptian labourers that work in most countries across the Arab world. The North African Arab countries – Tunisia, Morocco, Libya and Algeria – have a very different and distinct dialect that is not easily understood by other Arabs.

English is widely spoken across the Arab world and is the second language taught in schools and used by businesses.

---

9 See also 'Film and television production', page 199; and 'Music', page 200.

French is also taught and spoken in Lebanon and the Arab Maghreb countries.

Arabs are very proud of their rich language but are very aware of how difficult it is for a foreigner to learn it. So even though you are not expected to conduct business in Arabic, you will find a lot of appreciation and praise if you make the effort to learn to say a few useful phrases in Arabic – and even more, if you use the local dialect of the country you are in.

Chen Yi Xuan has found a fun way to learn the language: 'I love getting my fruit and vegetables from the fruit market in downtown, not from the supermarket. I learn my Arabic words from them. I hear them shout out the names of the fruits and vegetables they are selling and I see them, so I learn the words vividly from them. It makes the language alive.'

Meetings and correspondence will most likely be conducted in English; however, it is best not to make any assumptions, especially if you are dealing with a government entity. Double check beforehand so you can be prepared with your own translator or interpreter.

A good, trusted translator or interpreter can be expensive but, without a doubt, worth the investment. Look for someone who is experienced and can convey to you the tone and subtle meanings of what is being said. But you need to make sure that you remain in control of the situation and not allow your interpreter to negotiate on your behalf – something that might well happen, albeit in good faith.

Non-Arabs may notice that 'please' is not often used by Arabs when asking for something. A policeman or an immigration officer might say, 'Give me your passport,' or, 'I want your papers.' This can sound very rude and abrupt to a Western ear; however, rest assured that no offence is intended. In Arabic, the word 'please' is not often used but rather conveyed in other ways, including the tone of voice and the use of other phrases that are specific to each country.

Here are some useful words that can be used across the Arab world. Most are gender-neutral:

As salaamu alaykom
(Peace be upon you)

This is also referred to as the Islamic greeting.

Wa alaykom as salaam
(Peace be upon you also)

This is the response to the greeting.

Sabaah el khair
(Good morning)

Literally translated it means 'morning of blessings'.

Sabaah e-noor
(Morning of light)

This is the response to good morning.

Masaa el-khair
(Good evening)

Literally 'evening of blessings'.

Masaa el-noor
(Evening of light)

This is the response to 'good evening'.

Marhaba
(Hello, welcome)

Marhaba or **Marhabtain**
or **Ahlain**
(Two welcomes)

Ahlan wa sahlan
(Welcome)

Ahlan feek (for a male)
Ahlan feeki (for a female)
(Welcome to you)

Maa es salamah
(Goodbye)

Literally translated it means 'with safety'.

Shukran
(Thank you)

Afwan
(You are welcome)

This is the response to thank you.

Sahtain
(Double health)

This is similar to bon appetit, but is said before and after one eats.

Ala albak (for a male)
Ala albik (for a female)
(On your heart)

This is the response to *sahtain*. Meaning 'double health for your own heart'.

Maashallah
(Whatever God wants)

This expression is used when one sees something beautiful, such as a child.

Hamdilah
(Praise be to God)

This phrase is used often to give thanks to God for everything, to express gratitude.

Yalla
(Come on. Let's go)

Khalas
(Stop. Finish. Enough)

Tfadal **(for a male)**
(Used when someone is ushering you into a place or seat or handing you something)

Tfadali **(for a female)**

DECISIONS, RISKS AND CONTRACTS

Arab society in general is class conscious; they are comfortable with the fact that different people have their place and they are just treated differently. David, who comes from the UK, an egalitarian culture, is still getting used to that. 'To my ears, when they talk to their drivers or even some members of their staff it sounds very rough, but people actually don't mind. The person who – to my ears – is being shouted at, doesn't think anything of it, because he thinks that his job is to be given clear instructions. But to me it always jars.'

In egalitarian cultures bosses are often the first among equals. They are highly accessible and employees call them by their first name. But in the Arab world bosses are absolute authorities. The Arab business world is a very hierarchal culture that stems from its tribal and paternalistic nature. Power and decision-making is highly concentrated. Everything needs to come through the boss; he is the one who passes down instructions to his staff and all messages coming out of the organisation must come through him. It would be inappropriate for a middle-level younger person to question that authority.

Tari Lang has faced some difficulties with this aspect of the culture: 'There's a lot of agreeing to things because they want to agree with their bosses, and I don't think that's actually a helpful way to improve whatever it is that we are doing, because all the time you are worried that you have to say the right thing as far as what your boss thinks, rather than the right thing because it is the right thing to do. Although I do now understand the underlying reasons, it still frustrates me.'[1]

> ## Job titles
> Arabs in general attach a lot of weight and value to titles and positions. The appearance of authority and prestige is very important and so one would gladly accept a senior title even though the job does not actually carry any additional responsibilities or financial gain.

A DECISION IS MADE

Decisions in the Arab world are quite complex and involve a lot of people. The result is that responsibility and accountability is shared and spread out instead of being taken by one single person. So decisions are 'made', rather than 'taken'. This may appear to be at odds with such a hierarchal system, but if you recall, one of the main motivators for behaviour in Arab culture is avoiding shame, saving face and enhancing one's honour, as well as the importance of the family and reputation. Then this approach to making decisions makes sense.

Seeking 'consensus' and consulting others is a very important Islamic tradition. Hence committees are a regular part of the decision-making process, which is also a useful way for evading personal blame.[2]

---

1   See also 'Bad news', page 100, and 'Pleasing the boss', page 96.

2   See also 'The blame game', page 52.

The concept of *Shura*

Shura is the Arabic word meaning 'consultation', and is considered one of the main principles in Islam. It is a consultative decision-making process that is considered either obligatory or desirable by differing Islamic scholars.

In the Quran, two modes of political consultation are mentioned. In one, the Prophet Mohammed is asked to consult with his companions, but, ultimately, to decide on his own. In the other, the community of the faithful is described as the one that (among its other attributes) administers its affairs by mutual consultation. In the one, consultation is mandated but is not binding; in the other, it is depicted as constituting the very process by which binding decisions on public matters are reached.[3]

Shura remains a central issue in the ongoing political reform debate among Muslims.

The senior person making the decision depends on the reviews, technical evaluations and legal advice of his committees. He needs the support of the people around him to make sure that he is not making the wrong decision. So it is really an illusion of centralised control. It is not that there is someone sitting with the universal answer and you just need to get a meeting with that person to receive the decision that you want. Decisions take time because of this lengthy, inclusive process that involves a lot of people within the organisation who are, in their own way, shaping the final decision.

Saif has witnessed a number of Western companies lose business because of their total misunderstanding of how decisions are reached in this region. 'Some companies get a little

3   Sadek Jawad Sulaiman, Al Hewar Centre.

overconfident because they have a relationship with someone high up in the ranks. Unfortunately, they do not understand that everyone in the organisation provides his input, and the man on the top is not going to go against all his people; he will not risk his name for being thought of as the person who is getting paid under the table or dealing with any sort of unethical business by going against all that advice. So if you do not work it from the ground up, you won't get the deal.'

Eric has learned the importance of understanding the dynamics at work: 'You can influence it by finding the right messaging, the right packaging, finding a solution which is acceptable. And over time that solution emerges as the decision. So yes, it is hierarchical and you need to get the decision from the right person, but it is not that that person necessarily knows what the decision should be. It takes time and you really need to understand who are the influencers and the dynamics at play.'

It is quite rare for a difficult decision to arrive at the top of an organisation where one person has three options laid out in front of him and has to decide on which option to go with, which is then cascaded back into the organisation. Normally, by the time the options have reached the top person's desk, it is already clear which is the preferred choice; it has already kind of bubbled up, been socialised and agreed and everyone is on board. So it is, in reality, decision-making by soft consensus, where things slowly come together because no one person wants to take the risk.

Still, everything must get pushed up, and the decision will not pass until it has been signed off by the person at the top – even though it has been cooked elsewhere. And if the boss happens to be away, everything must wait until his return; it is very rare that someone would be willing to deputise and take action on behalf of the boss.

James Thomas discovered that through experience: 'That's why decisions take a long time, and why crazy things can work their way up through an organisation, because individual political and personal motivators are factored in as they go up. So some things can get to the top that are absolutely not commercial, not in the best interest of the organisation. Which would not happen if it was a top-down, commercially oriented organisation.'

Tony has found that he still falls in the trap of taking things for granted, particularly when he has worked with individuals in the region who are Western educated or lived abroad for a while. Such people are bi-cultural and can switch between the influences of their Arab culture and their Westernised education. 'I often don't know which mode a person is in when he is making a certain decision. It is very easy as an outsider to believe – oh I can deal with this person because they seem a lot like me, but in fact they might be making decisions in their local cultural mode rather than their Western, fluent English, highly articulated mode that you can easily take for granted. What I have tried to do is understand the constraints that they are working under to help me understand which mode they are likely to be in when they are trying to make a certain decision. If they are more in their local cultural context they would be much more concerned about relationships and who they are going to upset or offend by making this decision. But it is not easy for me as an outsider to know which of the competing priorities in their calculations is more important at that moment.'

Arabs tend to see relationships and connections between events, issues and objects – everything is somehow connected and nothing stands on its own. This mentality carries with it a risk – if everything is connected to everything else then a fairly simple and routine decision becomes incredibly complicated and difficult to make and so as a result, very little happens.

KEEPING THE BALANCE

The importance of maintaining some sort of balance is very important in the Arab mentality and the way decisions are made. This can be seen in both business and politics. Therefore, you will find that when a government announces a certain policy that will result in taking something away somewhere, the government will then feel the need to give it back somewhere else in order to somehow keep the balance. The same principal applies to appointments – especially in the public sector – where maintaining a balance between the different political and social powers becomes crucial.

Tony Goldner has found this need for balance and structure even in his dealings with people on a personal level: 'I have found that when a person does something that is confronting, there is then this strong desire to offset it by doing something nice so that you don't upset your relationship with that individual, because ultimately that may be someone you may need to call on in the future. So you don't want to burn bridges. Everyone likes to keep all their options open and their bridges accessible at all times.'

This, of course, makes it difficult to deal with the tough issues. And governments, in particular, would avoid making those tough binary decisions to avoid the risk of disrupting the balance or the risk of losing a relationship.

CAUTION AND RISK

In general, people in the Arab world will simply not take risks – they will actively avoid doing anything that may tarnish their reputation or bring shame to them or their family. That is why the phrase 'no objection' is so often used by those consulted, because it is safe and passive, unlike the more assertive phrase 'approved'.

For that reason, people will not buy something that hasn't already been tried by somebody else and that has been proven to work. Saif knows that too well: 'People here are not interested in any future business; they want something they know works. They want something they can see, feel and touch, that you can show them in a demonstration. They do not buy risk. If you say, "I will build it for you," they will say: "Build it and come back."'

As a result of this strong aversion to risk-taking, people in the Arab world tend to overlook the cost of inaction. So a piece of the overall equation is sometimes missing, and it becomes: 'I'd better not do something because five bad things may happen,' but there is not enough thinking around, 'What happens if I don't do anything?' This highly cautious approach and lack of cost–benefit thinking is the cause of quite a bit of frustration among foreigners working in the region.

Having said that, do not lose sight of the fact that Arabs are consummate traders and businessmen and are known for their enterprising spirit.

RULES AND REGULATIONS

Contrary to perceptions in the West, governments, companies and organisations in the Arab world have very detailed regulations, policies and rules that cover every activity. Entering into a contract or submitting a tender requires strict adherence to every step in that company's procedures policy. There is no getting around it.

Dan Monaghan has found the bureaucracy a bit overwhelming: 'Everything requires some sort of permit or licence. If we want to do any kind of business promotion, we have to get a permit. If we need to get some work done overnight, we have to get police permits to allow the workers to work overnight. Especially in Dubai, there's a lot of paperwork and the customs department is very strict. If, for example, we have a shipment coming in and the paperwork says 100 tonnes of clothing without specifying the brands, it can get held up for a month until the detailed paperwork is presented.'

Saif faces these misperceptions frequently: 'When a company is bringing equipment into the country, it needs to have the proper papers. I have had people say to me: "Well, you are in the region, you know people, call someone and get the shipment through." I find that shocking. I would never ask him to do that in the US or the UK, so why would he ask me to do it here? I understand this is the Middle East, but it is not lawless land. There are laws, there are regulations and procedures. It is not this unknown territory where anything goes.'

PUTTING IT INTO CONTEXT

One of the key differences among cultures is the attitude people have towards rules and laws. In the rules-based cultures of the West, laws and rules are made to apply uniformly to all parties in all situations. Nevertheless, case law and legal interpretations allow both individuals and organisations to push the limits of what is permissible.

In the Arab world the attitude towards rules, policies and laws is mixed and can be seen as 'for our friends we interpret the law and for our enemies we apply the law'. The general attitude of Arab culture towards laws and regulations is that they were created to serve people and the relationship. The value of the relationship – in many cases – outweighs the value of upholding the rule and the process. Here the 'context' is significant. Remember that the Arab world is a relationships-based culture; therefore, the context, the people involved and their relationship play a role in determining whether a rule is applied or bent in that particular situation.[4]

This point of view became clear to Jayne a little too late. I met Jayne – a highly qualified English-language teacher – in Dubai, where she was teaching at one of the local universities after moving there from Kuwait. Jayne shared an experience she had had with the owner of the school she worked for in Kuwait. 'At that time,' she explained, 'the rules were that in

4   See also 'Relationships and trust', page 54; '*The wasta*', page 65.

order for me to qualify for a higher grade and a higher salary, I had to have specific academic qualifications, which I did, but I also had to have at least ten years of practical teaching experience. My practical experience fell six months short of the ten years' requirement. This came up during an appraisal meeting with the director and owner of the school where I had been working for over two years; he said that my performance had been excellent and that he could overlook the rule and state that I had the ten-year practical experience that would entitle me to a raise.'

Jayne recalled her reaction: 'I was shocked. I interpreted his suggestion as an insult; how could he ask me to lie and break the rules? His reaction to my reaction was confusion and of course he, too, was insulted that I had accused him of being a liar. The relationship – which prior to that incident was very good – quickly deteriorated, and shortly after that I left that job.'

After a few minutes of reflection, Jayne went on, 'It took me a few years to understand what my boss in Kuwait was trying to do and where he was coming from. Now I understand the importance of relationships in the culture and how people, in many cases, outweigh the importance of procedures and rules. If I knew that then, my reaction would have been very different. He was just trying to help me.'

Having lived in the region for many years, Tony Goldner seems to have developed an understanding to this issue: 'I think there are some laws that people would not dare to cross, because they understand that the consequences would be dramatic – you can be arrested, you can be charged, you can be fined – but I think too many of the rules and regulations are not properly enforced, and so people learn which ones are hard and which ones are soft. I have found that people here are inclined towards avoiding the soft rules rather than following them. This is evident in people's attitude towards traffic laws, littering and smoking in public buildings.'

Foreigners and the law
As a foreigner in an Arab country, make sure you abide by the law of the land. While locals may be able to get away with bending a few rules and with *wasta*, as a foreigner you will not get the same breaks.

CONTRACTS
Typically, rules-focused societies, such as the US and Western Europe, enter agreements using very detailed and lengthy contracts. Every aspect of the relationship is set and governed by the signed contract. In contrast, in the Arab world, contracts tend to be much shorter and are regarded as merely a written record of what has been discussed and agreed upon. The relationship is not governed by the contract.

Tony Goldner found this to be a particularly significant area of difference in the cultures: 'Here, even if you sign a contract, the attitude is that it is still up for renegotiation if you need it to be. Consequently, that makes people from other cultures nervous that the rules of the game could suddenly change on them and they could be asked to do a lot more. So it cuts to different notions of trust – what does trust mean, and how do you create a common platform of trust to allow people from different cultural backgrounds to engage with one another?'

Alexis McGinness was surprised by this aspect: 'There is always a lot of interesting bargaining. They have signed off on something, but then – we can still bargain on it. Nothing is firm. In the context of my organisation it is firm, but there's always the post-signature bargaining that occurs.'

The honour-based culture of the Arab world relies more heavily on one's word of honour, reputation and relationships rather than written documentation – although documents are important and are kept. But if either party starts referring to the contract, that is a sign that the relationship has failed.

Graham Ball realised the importance of focusing on strengthening the personal relationship: 'The most important thing about contracts in this part of the world, other than to have one, is don't have a lot of faith in it. It is far, far more important that you build up a level of trust and understanding with the individual rather than to say, "Well, I have got a contract, therefore I have this wonderful fortress around me and if anything goes wrong I can go to court with it."'

Taking contractual disagreements to court is definitely not the preferred option for many reasons – least of which is the lengthy and complicated legal process. You need to be aware of all the other dynamics at play. In the West, making something public is a card that you would use to your advantage. You would mobilise public opinion in support of your outcome. But in this part of the world, if you make things public, you have automatically created a situation where someone would lose face[5] openly, bringing shame to everyone and

5   See 'Directness and saving face', page 88.

everything that person represents. It is far more prudent to find ways of resolving disagreements in private, working your way to a solution that is acceptable to both sides.

With more and more international business being conducted in the Arab world and with the younger Western-educated generation, the mindset around adhering to contracts has been shifting. In Dubai, in particular, they have moved beyond the traditional way of relying on personal connections and are more focused on contracts and clear documentation. Now RFPs (requests for proposal) from government departments are well documented and all the procedures are very clear.

THE CONCEPT OF TIME

Perhaps it is the nature of life in the desert. Or perhaps it is the strong belief in fate and that everything is in the hands of our creator;[1] the attitude towards the concept of time in the Arab world is more flexible and fluid in comparison to the more schedule-oriented and punctual cultures of North America and Western Europe. An Arab may say, 'I will see you before one hour,' or, 'I will see you after two days.' The first means that it will not be longer than an hour before he sees you, and in the second instance, it will be at least two days.

Although things are changing – and the younger generation is much more inclined towards Western business practices of scheduling and timekeeping – still the underlying attitude towards the concept of time remains different from the West and is therefore perhaps the issue that most frustrates non-Arabs working and living in the region.

Jonghee Son found this aspect very different from her own South Korean culture: 'In Korea, everywhere you go you will always hear people say quick, quick. Here everywhere you go you hear *shway, shway* [Arabic word meaning "slowly"].'

---

1 See also 'Faith and fate', page 66.

Tari Lang, too, found herself having to cope with these differences when she took up a contract in the Gulf: 'Timekeeping, or rather the lack of, is one of the things that I found annoying. People being late, appointments being changed at the last minute. However, I kept thinking, I am working in somebody else's country; I am taking somebody else's dollar, I need to be as sensitive as possible to the way that somebody else works, I need to be more patient than normal. So therefore I was much more lenient and forgiving in the sort of things that were done. Had it happened to me in London for example, my reaction would have been different.'

Felix Bernhard – a German working in Jordan – had a similar attitude: 'I am a guest here, so I cannot expect the people around me to go by my rules, but I cannot change myself. For example, if I make an appointment at my apartment to repair something and the people say they will be there at five, I do not expect them to be there at five, but it still bugs me if they are ten minutes late. And if they are any more than fifteen minutes late, I am on the phone chasing them. But I found that in the office, people are on time and stick to schedules – at least, that is my experience in Jordan.'

Giovanna Negretti, on the other hand, coming from a Latino culture, found that the Arabs' concept of time was very similar to hers: 'When we say four o'clock, we really mean six. Lateness is not something that we think about.'

TIME OR PEOPLE?

'Time is money. Time is precious. Make the most of it.' This is a belief that is ingrained in the cultures of most of Europe,

North America, Canada and Australia. For those cultures, time set aside for an activity that doesn't happen is time wasted that can never be reclaimed or recovered.

People from a schedule-oriented culture measure success or achievement by the number of meetings completed in a day, and whether or not everything went as scheduled and all meetings finished at the exact time allotted. Last-minute changes and ad hoc events would mess up your entire schedule and cause you a fair degree of stress. Time-oriented people have their diaries planned weeks and even months in advance, with very little room for flexibility.

On the other hand, if you were from the people-oriented cultures of the Arab world, South America and the Mediterranean, then your approach to time would be much more flexible, and achievement might be measured by how effectively you were able to handle last-minute cancellations and changes, all the while giving priority to people in your situation or setting. In this culture, a schedule may serve as a general guideline and is often replaced with a list of people that one needs to see and things that need to be done. For a time-oriented person, this may appear chaotic, inefficient and frustrating, while the planning style of the time-oriented person may appear to be too cold and rigid to someone from a people-oriented culture.

Take the Arab minister or senior official who walks out of his office to find a waiting room full of people who want to see him for a variety of issues. As he leaves to get to his next meeting in another location, he spends roughly twenty minutes going around the room answering questions, signing documents, resolving problems or giving instructions to his staff to follow up on more complex issues. Within a short span of time, the official is able to respond to the needs of several people at once. 'If you value people, you must hear them out; you cannot cut them off simply because of a schedule, even if it means being a few minutes late to the next appointment.' The focus is on the people, and the schedule becomes secondary. Everyone is happy.

Walk into a shop or marketplace in the Arab world and you will find yourself surrounded by other customers all competing for the attention of the salesperson, who is trying to cater to everyone all at once. There is no queue or numbers to indicate who has been waiting the longest, but somehow, surprisingly, things move along at a reasonably quick pace, and everyone is happy.

Again, there is no right or wrong, just different – different approaches, different perspectives and different ways of organising time. One approach is events scheduled as separate items – one thing at a time – as in North Europe and North America, and the other is several things at once. Each system has a different logic; each system has its strengths and weaknesses, and, like oil and water, they don't mix.[2]

IS IT WASTING TIME?
In the Arab world, too, time is valued, but so are relationships and enjoying life. An Arab saying illustrates this well: 'You [Westerners] have the watches, we have the time.'

---

2   Edward T. Hall. *The Dance of Life*, Anchor Books edition, 1989.

In the West, a meeting would immediately turn to business, but in many other countries, including the Arab world, people will spend time talking about general topics while sipping on a cup of Arabic coffee or mint tea, to get to know each other better, to build the relationship and break the ice before slowly turning to business. Is this a waste of time?

'I felt very offended.' Ahmad, the patriarch of a Jordanian family business, recalled his interaction with an American business owner with whom his company was negotiating a major construction contract. 'I phoned him one time, and just a few seconds into the call, he says, "What can I do for you?"' Ahmad went on to explain: 'I didn't want anything from him, I just wanted to ask after him and to chat. For me the conversation in itself is valuable, but I got the impression that I was wasting his time. After that I was very reluctant to call him again.'

Don't lose sight of the fact that Arabs attach great value to building and nurturing relationships.[3] Business is built on relationships. And Arabs do take business personally and would, more often than not, put the relationship above any other consideration. Here, time is seldom experienced as 'wasted'.

Jonghee Son had to learn the value of this: 'Here when you have a meeting you have to first sit and you wait and drink coffee and tea and talk. I would be burning, but I had to sit. But now that I have built the relationship and they know me, I can say, "Okay five minutes and then we get to work." Now I can get away with doing that and they accept me.'

---

3   See also 'Relationships and trust', page 54.

Patience is also a virtue that is highly regarded by the Arabs. One is encouraged to take time to ponder, contemplate and to allow for things to settle or work themselves out before rushing into a decision that could bring shame to himself and his people. Rushing your Arab counterpart and demanding an immediate decision or response will be counterproductive.[4]

FLEXIBILITY AND THE RIGHT TIMING

Scheduling meetings and planning business trips – especially to the Gulf countries – must be approached with a completely different state of mind. Quick in-and-out trips will not work here. You need to be flexible and to give yourself extra time. You may even find yourself boarding the flight to Saudi, Doha or the UAE with nothing confirmed in your diary except a note from the Arab executive or official you are going to meet, saying: 'Call me when you are here.'

Saif experiences these issues on a daily basis: 'I get emails from some very high-level people from the US saying I am arriving Tuesday and leaving Wednesday evening, would you set up meetings with x, y and z. They don't understand that it doesn't work that way. We must first *request* the meeting and then talk about a date and time. Travel plans should be made after we have the agreement for the meeting.'

Eric has found a way to manage this difference: 'What I do is to have more than one thing working in parallel. What usually takes a quarter from start to finish in the West, here would take years until you get to the point where you can start the quarter,

---

4   See also 'A decision is made', page 120; and 'Directness and saving face', page 88.

then it takes a quarter here as well.' After years of working in the region, Eric totally understands that it is more a question of getting alignment, building consensus and comfort around what needs to be done, and that takes time. 'What it means is that you will have to build different timelines. They are what they are; you can impact them by being more intelligent about finding the right answer and the right approach. A solution that is helpful and creates winners.'

Timing is everything. Arabs in general are quite observant and will wait until the person is in the right mood to listen so they get the positive response they are after. An Arab would pick up information and certain signs and would be able to sense the best time to approach that person – even if it means waiting for a few days. Rushing it would be foolish and would risk a negative response that could mean even longer delays.

Weekends and public holidays

Before you start planning for a business trip make sure you are aware of any public holidays. Friday is the sacred day and is spent with the family. No work will be done on Fridays. The weekend in all the Arab countries (including Saudi since 2013) is Friday and Saturday. The exceptions are Lebanon and Tunisia, where it is Saturday and Sunday.

There is no point in scheduling half-hour meetings or appointments that are too close to each other. Be prepared for delays – meetings rarely start on time and there will likely be a number of interruptions. It is quite common for the person you are meeting with to decide to introduce you to someone else who might be interested in your proposal, and would very likely just pick up the phone or take you to that person's office on the spur of the moment. Avoid requesting meetings too close to the lunch break and be aware of prayer times.[5]

Again, do not forget that individuals differ and the younger generation has more of a Western businesslike approach to meetings and schedules.

MANY THINGS AT ONCE

In Arab culture, everything appears to be in a constant state of fluidity, nothing is solid or firm – and even the most important plans can be changed at the very last minute. Again, the focus is on the people and completing the transaction rather than sticking to the schedule.

Graham Ball explained his surprise when he first started working in the Arab world: 'I found myself struggling at first to adjust to the way many Lebanese attempt to multitask in a way that to me appears totally chaotic. They seem to find it hard to give you or anything their undivided focused attention for any length of time. But this is only the perception through UK eyes. I later realised that they were not being intentionally disrespectful and would probably have been horrified that I had thought so. It took me some time to get used to it, though. I would be in a meeting, and my counterpart's phone would ring or a text message would arrive, and he would break off and take the call or answer the message. Equally, they're not concerned if I do the same. I simply learned to be patient and to just wait for the meeting and our conversation to resume.'

---

5   See 'Five daily prayers', page 74.

Trish, an American consultant who has been working in the region, told me that she had somehow managed to adjust to this sense of fluidity in her work schedule but still got frustrated with her hairdresser, Majdi. She had regular appointments confirmed in her diary twice a week at 4 p.m. But every time she arrived at her scheduled appointment exactly on time, she would find that Majdi had 'squeezed in' another one of his customers. Trish was understandably aggravated.

I explained to her the kind of pressure and expectations that the culture puts on Majdi and others. He has to be always ready to accommodate last-minute requests from customers, friends and relatives to demonstrate the importance of those relationships to him. However, he would try to make it up to Trish by spending a little extra time on styling her hair or maybe even using a special product without charging her. His aim is to somehow find a balance and to keep everyone happy.

PLANS AND PLANNING

In the West, a great amount of time and effort is spent on planning every detail and preparing for any eventuality. It is the norm for someone from the West to plan a family vacation a year in advance. The dates are set in the calendar, the tickets are purchased and all the hotel bookings are confirmed months in advance. From an Arab point of view, that would be unheard of. Planning so far ahead in this manner has an element of tempting fate. So it is common to hear an Arab use such phrases as: 'If we were still alive next summer, then we would think about doing this.' One would intend for something to happen, then leave the rest in the hands of the Almighty.[6]

This, undoubtedly, has a significant impact on the way businesses are run in the Arab world. James Thomas is struggling hard with the company he is working with to get them to shift their focus from what they need to deliver this year to building a meaningful three-to-five year plan with detailed, challenging goals, targets and activities. 'Planning is viewed as an academic exercise that is done outside the business, while their focus remains on solving today's problems.'

There are, of course, many reasons behind that attitude – the chaotic political situation in some Arab countries undoubtedly plays a role. The frequent change of officials and lack of continuity is another. Religion, too, plays a role here. While Western cultures are largely secular, in the Arab world religion and the state are very much intertwined. Islam dictates a way of life and has a very strong influence over beliefs and values in Arab culture. Central to the Islamic faith and therefore to the Arab outlook on life, is the concept of *qada'a wa qadar* – fate and God's will.[7]

PERCEPTION OF DEADLINES

In Germany, it is very common to hear an announcement notifying travellers that the train will be one minute late. In France, the term *le quart d'heure de politesse* actually encourages people not to be on time. In China it is acceptable to miss a deadline, while in Spain, there is no exact translation for the word deadline.

---

6   See also 'Faith and fate', page 66. '*Inshallah*', page 68.

7   See also 'Faith and fate', page 66.

The Arabs, like many other so-called *mañana* cultures, are a lot more relaxed about deadlines and generally have little understanding of the need to rush. An American business-man tells the story of how stressed he was about getting his Arab colleague to abide by the deadline for delivering a con-struction project his company was working on in one of the Arabian Gulf countries; his Arab partner replied: 'My country has been living without this building for the past fifty years; it can continue to do so for another couple of weeks.'

Eric has learned that the best way to cope with this difference is not to worry about some of the things you would normally worry about in the West: 'I have learned not to get too wor-ried about the start dates and deadlines. Find an agreement on what you need to get done; once you have that, either things will have happened on the client's side or you can bring it up in a discussion and find the best solution to get things done.'

Graham Ball is still trying to grasp the concept: 'My under-standing of the word *bukra* [the Arabic word for 'tomorrow'] means sometime in the future. So I really cannot understand the concept of *ba'ad bukra* [Arabic for 'after tomorrow']. How can you have something that is after some time in the future?? So if somebody then says: *ba'ad bukra inshallah*,[8] I would panic, because to me that means it's never going to happen. But somehow it always seems to happen.'

---

8 See also '*Inshallah*', page 68.

IT'S URGENT

The Arabs' concept of time is very much focused on the now, the short-term; therefore actions tend to be reactive and things tend to happen at short notice. It is therefore, perfectly normal for you to get a call saying, 'Can you come now? We can sit and discuss the proposal you have.'

Tony Goldner has found difficulty in understanding this aspect of the culture: 'I think the hardest thing to reconcile is that sometimes things are in an incredible hurry and have to be done much faster than people would normally do them anywhere else, and yet at other times there's no rush at all and it's almost impossible to understand why something is suddenly in a hurry or why it can wait for six months. And sometimes the two things happen one after the other: we have to have this meeting tomorrow and then nothing happens for six months. It's like hurry up and wait, or just wait.'

One needs to keep in mind that there are always many factors at play that are most likely not evident to a foreigner. Patience would serve you well here.

Dan Monaghan, too, was frustrated with the speed of business in some of the countries he worked in, like Kuwait and Jordan: 'For me the overuse of the word *inshallah*[9] in business was something I had trouble with until I really understood what *inshallah* meant. For me, when I first came to Kuwait, it meant basically, "If I want to do it, I'm going to do it." But there was no sense of urgency – "So I'm going to drink my tea, I'm

---

9 See also '*Inshallah*', page 68.

going to smoke my cigarette, I'm going to do whatever else I need to do before it happens."'

Pacing is another consideration. The different rates of speed that people are accustomed to in different cultures. Victoria, an account manager at a multinational firm based out of New York, found it difficult to get prompt responses from one of her partner companies in Saudi Arabia. The schedule-oriented, fast-paced Victoria was clearly frustrated: 'I think it is perfectly reasonable to send an email to my counterpart in the Saudi company asking for some specific information which I need by the end of the week. The information I was asking for was not difficult and I really think two days is a very generous deadline.'

I explained to Victoria that in order for her to get her desired response, she would need to consider several factors:

1. Bureaucracy and the decision-making process in that organisation will influence how quickly things get done.[10]

2. The tone of the request must not come across as a demand – employees will listen only to their direct boss.

3. Provide some more details and background as to why she needs that information and why the sense of urgency.

TIME AS STATUS
Time is also a symbol of status. The amount of leeway an individual gets in any given time system is an indication of

---

10   See also 'A decision is made', page 121.

that person's position in an organisation or society. How long can one keep others waiting for an appointment? How quickly can one get a transaction completed, despite the bureaucracy? These are very important indications of the status of that person, his relationships and connections. While waiting one's turn is one of the basic points in North European and American cultures (the Brits having refined queuing to a national art), in the mentality of Arab culture, the connection and relationship are more important than who has been waiting in line the longest. Although the ticket number system was introduced in most public departments in an attempt to employ best practice and a more efficient system for delivery of services, most people across the Arab world still find it difficult to queue in an orderly manner, waiting for their turn, and have no qualms about side-stepping the system.

TIME AND THE PAST

To the Arabs, history and tradition are an integral part of their identity. Children grow up listening to stories of their elders and they learn the names of the heroes in their tribe and nation. They know that where they are today is part of a historical trail that connects them with their family, their tribe, their nation.

In contrast, the American culture, for example, is quick to discard the old and eager to clasp the new. As Edward T. Hall notes, this is reflected in their attitudes towards ideas, books and music. 'It is as if there are deep unconscious patterns that encourage them to automatically disavow the old, which breaks the thread of continuity'.[11]

---

11   Edward T. Hall, *The Dance of Life*, Anchor Books edition, 1989, page 87.

Arabs, in general, like to talk about history, especially things that are shared or held in common with the history of their non-Arab guests. David, a diplomat living in Cairo, says: 'Often we don't remember as Westerners the amount of history that comes with the relationship between the West and the Arab world. We have much shorter memories than Arab people do.' Some elements of that history are good, but there are also some that are perceived very negatively. 'I think people in the Arab world feel they have sometimes been the victims of a lot of outside interference – pushed around a lot, so they are very sensitive to whether they are being shown understanding and respect. Especially Arab Muslims, who feel they have lost a place in the world as a great civilisation and they no longer have that preeminent status.'

Almost everywhere you go across the Arab world, you will get this sense of tension of two forces pulling in different directions – one towards modernisation and change and the other holding on to history and traditions. In many cases, you will be able to sense this tension not only manifesting itself clearly on the outside but also within the same individual. Today, the younger Western-educated generation across the Arab world is pushing for change. However, there remains a strong resistance to this drive towards modernisation out of fear of losing the Arab identity and ending up as replicas of the West.

8

ETIQUETTE, PROTOCOL AND

HOSPITALITY

It is said that an Arab is known to have five main traits or characteristics that are rooted in the Bedouin traditions and values. These are:

1. Physiognomy: the art of discovering a person's temperament and character from facial expressions and outward appearance.

2. Hospitality to guests: generosity is a very important and desirable trait for the Arabs.

3. Forgiveness when possible: the ability for a person to forgive someone who has wronged him, even though he has the ability to enforce punishment.

4. Providing relief, help and assistance for those in need of it: also known as chivalry.

5. Providing aid to those who have lost the ability to earn their own livelihood.

You will find these characteristics still make up the core values in the Arabs' beliefs and their social interactions, not only among each other but also with their guests and visitors.

NAMES, TITLES AND FORMS OF ADDRESS

An Arab person's name can tell a whole story: a person's history, where he fits in that society, the geographic region his family is originally from, his religion, and in many cases also the political affiliations. Many families are connected – some tracing their origins to the same tribe, others through intermarriages. Branches of the same family can also be found spread out in different Arab countries.

A person's name in the Arab world is made of four or five segments. It starts with the person's given name, followed by the father's name, the paternal grandfather's name, then the family name and, finally, the name of the tribe the family belongs to. For example, in Ahmad Ali Abdullah Alsafi bani Hassan, Ahmad is the given name, Ali is his father's name, Abdullah is Ahmad's grandfather's name, Alsafi is the family name and bani Hassan is the name of the tribe that family belongs to.

Bin or *bani* means 'the son of' So Hussein bin Talal literally means 'Hussein, the son of Talal'. The bani Hashem tribe is 'the sons of Hashem tribe'. And for females, *bint* means 'the daughter of'. So Princess Raya bint Abdullah bin Al-Hussein bani Hashem is 'Raya, the daughter of Abdullah, who is the son of Hussein, the son of the Hashem tribe'.

Almost all first names in the Arab world carry a meaning in the Arabic language or have a religious Islamic significance. For example, Abdullah means the servant/slave of Allah (God), Abdulaziz means the servant/slave of the honourable and very dear (Aziz is one of the ninety-nine names that are given to God in Islam).

Arabs are very conscious of protocol and proper procedures as an expression of respect. Therefore, it is almost always better to err on the side of caution and formality when addressing an Arab, because if you make the mistake of starting off too informally, chances are they will not correct you, but they will feel it and it can damage the relationship. It is therefore best to avoid addressing someone by their first name until you are specifically asked to do so.

Arabs are very proud of their official titles and like to use them often. So if the person has an official position, you should use 'Your Excellency' when speaking to him or 'His Excellency' when referring to him. Doctor or Engineer are also used. And if the person does not have a formal title, you could address him as Mr Abdullah (using his first name), until he asks you to call him by his first name only.

Military titles should always be used when addressing a member of the armed forces. In some Arab countries – Jordan, Syria, Lebanon, Palestine and Egypt – titles inherited from the Turks are still in use – such as *baik* or *basha*.[1] These are used after a person's first name and are meant to show rank and respect, for example, Aziz *baik* or Aziz *basha*.

---

1   Basha is the title used for the highest civilian and military ranks of Marshall, General and Major General.

Coming from the UK, Peter Millett found he had to get used to this kind of formality. 'In the UK everything is becoming increasingly less formal. We just don't use "Your Excellency". We would call a minister "Minister" if you are meeting for the first time and then you would use his first name. Whereas for the Arabs it is important. People here always refer to me as Your Excellency. It is, after all, them showing respect and giving me the honour they think I am looking for.'

Another form of showing respect – which is widely used across the Arab world and across all social classes – especially when addressing an older woman, and in order to avoid using her first name (which is considered inappropriate in the more conservative Arab societies) is the term *Umm* followed by the name of the eldest son (or the eldest daughter if the woman doesn't have any sons), which means mother of 'X'. So it would be Umm Ahmad – meaning mother of Ahmad. And for a male it would be Abu Ahmad – meaning father of Ahmad.

Having lived here for a few years, Giovanna Negretti enjoys the fact that when she goes to the Starbucks next to her house, they know her and call her Umm Maya, 'I just love it! And they know what Umm Maya drinks. I just love that feeling of belonging and community.'

In a business setting, you need to be cautious, though, that this can show a certain level of familiarity. So the best course of action for you is to be formal and use Mr – or any other formal title that the person may hold – combined with the first name. You may also ask others who work with that senior person how he prefers to be addressed.

Sheikh (pronounced 'shake', not 'sheek') – is another title that has several uses. It is the title given for an elderly religious Muslim cleric. It is also the title given to a tribal leader. And in the Arabian Gulf, it is the title used for members of the royal family. You would not say, 'Good morning, Sheikh.' The correct way is to say: 'Good morning, Sheikh Mohammed.' Sheikha is the female version.

Titles of Arab heads of state

Jordan, Bahrain, Morocco, Saudi Arabia: King (addressed as Your Majesty).

Kuwait, Qatar: Emir (addressed as Your Highness).

Oman: Sultan (addressed as Your Highness).

Egypt, Lebanon, Palestine, Syria, Libya, Tunisia, Algeria and Yemen: President (addressed as Your Excellency).

The King of Saudi Arabia is honoured with the ancient title 'Custodian of the Two Holy Mosques'. Caring for the holy cities of Mecca, the birthplace of Islam and the Prophet Mohammed, and Medina, the Prophet's burial place, is a sacred trust exercised on behalf of all Muslims. Recognising the unique and historic tradition these holy sites represent, the King of Saudi Arabia adopted the official title of the Custodian of the Two Holy Mosques as an expression of his deep sense of responsibility toward Islam.

Hajj or *Hajji* is a title used for someone who has performed the Muslim pilgrimage to Mecca[2]. It can also be used to express respect while addressing an old man. *Hajjeh* is the female version.

---

2   See also 'The Hajj', page 82.

GREETINGS

The most common greeting in the Arab world in all circumstances is the handshake. This must be done while standing up, coupled with eye contact and the exchange of a word of greeting such as, '*As salaamu alaykom.*'[3]

You must shake hands when you first enter and also at the end of the meeting. You are expected to do that even if you have a meeting with the same person more than once in the same day. If you are sitting in a room or office, you must stand up when a person walks in – especially if that person has a senior position or is older.

Business cards

Business cards are given during the conversation with no ceremony. It is advisable to have one side of your business card in English and the other in Arabic. Some foreign names may come out strangely when written in Arabic, so make sure that you get someone to proof-read it before printing.

The handshake may be more prolonged than in Western countries, and may include enquiries about your health and well-being. Greetings should not be rushed. It is important to take time to exchange social pleasantries during the greeting process – enquire about his health and the family and children (but not the wife).[4]

If you are a man greeting an Arab woman, wait until she extends her hand first. A Muslim woman may prefer not to shake hands with a man and would instead place her right

---

3   See 'Useful Arabic words', page 117.

4   See also 'The family is private', page 33.

hand over her heart and very slightly bow her head as a greeting gesture.

If you are a woman, a Muslim man may choose not to have any physical contact and would therefore put his right hand over his heart. Take a moment to read the situation and the body language; if he does not put out his hand, then you can simply put your right hand over your heart while saying a word of greeting with a smile and a slight nod of the head to show respect and acknowledgement. If you put out your hand and he responds by putting his right hand on his heart, simply do the same and don't feel any embarrassment or stress.

The handshake was one of the first things that Alexis McGinness learned when she came to the Middle East: 'I had also worked in Los Angeles with Orthodox Jews who would not shake hands with a woman. My boss had explained it to me, so I was prepared and did not get offended, because I knew not to stick out my hand and make a fool of myself. Having those previous experiences helped me understand.'

Like many Westerners new to the region, Felix Bernhard experienced this somewhat embarrassing situation: 'I was at a function and I saw an Arab colleague who works with me. We greeted each other in a friendly manner, but I had not met his wife before, so I wanted to shake hands with her, but I did not understand her body language.

> ### Greeting groups of people
>
> Precedence is given to rank and then age. When you enter a group, you must show respect to the eldest person by greeting him/her first.

She started backing off and I felt very embarrassed. I wasn't prepared for this experience.'

Family, friends or close acquaintances of the same sex may greet each other with a handshake and a brief kiss on each cheek, starting with the right side. But there are also several other forms of greeting kisses that are specific to certain countries and also depend on the relationship – i.e. father to son, or senior person to junior person, or ruler to citizen.[5]

An older man may kiss the forehead of his son; a citizen may kiss the top of the shoulder of his ruler as a sign of respect. In the Gulf countries the 'nose kiss' is common, where a man slightly touches the tip of his nose to the tip of the nose of another man in greeting. In Lebanon, the norm is three kisses – starting from the right, then left, then right again; while in Jordan it starts with one kiss on the right then one, two or three on the left side. Unlike some Western and Latino cultures, hugging is not a common part of greetings in the Arab world.

Signs of friendship

It is quite common, especially in the Gulf countries, to see two Arab males walking together while gently holding hands without any embarrassment. This is not an indication of anything other than a simple friendship. This is less common among females, although you may see two women walking in public with their arms linked. Again, this is not an indication of anything other than a close friendship.

It is expected and considered polite to say a word of greeting when you walk into a room or you pass colleagues at the office.

---

5   See also 'Socialising with the opposite sex', page 178.

'This was something that came up in our office – we are a total of about ninety people – the issue of not saying good morning to everybody.' Alexis did not think it was important, but then realised that it was all about the little things and how they are interpreted as gestures of respect. 'So now, even though I am half asleep in the morning, I make sure I say good morning to everyone I pass in the office.'

APPEARANCE AND DRESS CODES

Appearance is very important, and Arabs in general – both men and women – do make an effort with their clothing and personal grooming. Dress codes for Arab nationals differ from one region to the other. In the Levant, Iraq, Egypt and the Arab Maghreb countries, Western-style clothing is the norm for both men and women, except for women who choose to follow the Islamic dress code, which is the *hijab* or the *niqab*. Tribal leaders and people living in some of the towns and cities outside the capital might also choose to wear their national dress instead of Western-style clothing.

Women from all the Arabian Gulf countries – except for Kuwait and Bahrain – are required to wear an *abaya* and cover their hair when they are in public. The *abaya* is a cloak-like garment made from a black fabric, which the woman wears over her regular clothes as a sign of modesty. This dress code is the strictest in Saudi Arabia and is regularly enforced by the *mutawaa*.[6]

Most foreigners coming to the Arab world are struck by how fashionable and trendy most Arab women are. All the high-end

6 See 'Unique to Saudi Arabia', page 78.

designer brands, as well as the well-known street fashion brands, are sold in almost all the Arab capitals. Women here take pride in their appearance and make an effort to look good. They follow the latest fashion and world trends as reported in numerous international and Arabic fashion magazines and television programmes.

Men in the Gulf wear a long garment called a *dishdash*, also referred to as *thoub* or *kandoura* and a headdress known as *shmakh* or *hatta*. Men in the Gulf in particular care a lot about their appearance and personal grooming. They prefer to dye their grey hair black and they are always well shaven with their beards trimmed (except for religious clerics, who let their beards grow long and untrimmed).

As a foreigner, you should present yourself well, as you will be judged by your appearance. A good-quality business suit in navy blue or dark grey with a white or light blue shirt and a conservative-style tie is the safest way to go, especially for first-time meetings. Social intelligence requires that you respect the local conservative social values and dress and behave in the appropriate manner. Going out in shorts, tank tops and flip-flops – even for men – is generally frowned upon. Arabs are very forgiving of foreigners and will not say anything. But look around you; if you are the only one in that style of clothing then you might want to reconsider your choice.

As a Western woman, modesty is essential – in both clothing and behaviour. Shoulders should be covered; arms to the elbow, and in the more conservative Gulf countries, arms need to be covered to the wrist. Hemlines should be at least to the knee. In Saudi Arabia, all women – regardless of nationality

– are required to wear the *abaya* and also cover their hair when going out in public places. Foreign women are not required to wear the *abaya* or cover their hair in any other Arab country.

Giovanna Negretti, coming from the Latino beach culture of Puerto Rico, found difficulty in getting used to the stricter dress codes when she first moved to the region: 'I come from a culture where we are in shorts and tank tops all the time, so it took me time to get used to not being able to dress that way here, in order to be respectful of this culture but also for me to get the respect that I want from the people around me.' Still, Giovanna did find one similarity with her own culture: 'My mother always told me, almost since the day I was born, that as long as a woman has her hair and nails done, everything else is fine. I was so surprised to find that all the woman here have that same obsession with their hair and nails.'

PUBLIC SAFETY
Crime rates in the Arab world are generally low in comparison with other parts of the world. Most are petty crimes and theft that are not related to organised crime.

As a foreign woman you are totally safe walking on the streets of most Arab capital cities. However, use your common sense and judgement and be aware of what you are wearing, the time of day or night and whether you are walking alone in a deserted neighbourhood or a main street. And of course, when in doubt, ask a local person for their advice.

Harassment of women on the street varies from one country to the other and ranges from harmless comments of admiration thrown from a distance to other more threatening approaches. The severity of punishment for such harassment also varies from one country to the other. In the UAE, for example, any man caught harassing a woman is named and shamed in the public media; and if that man is an expat, he faces immediate deportation.

In the Arab world people treasure the opportunity of interacting with a foreigner and getting to know them. Therefore, do not be alarmed if people come up to you and start a conversation that may well end up with an invitation for a cup of mint tea or a coffee. Arabs are genuinely curious people and like to show their hospitality and generosity to guests. Needless to say, you should use your judgement before accepting an invitation to a complete stranger's home.

RULES ON THE ROAD
Driving on the roads of most of the countries in the Arab world is an art and a game of survival. One-way street signs and 'no parking' signs are regularly ignored, and in places like Beirut and Cairo a red traffic light is often taken as a mere suggestion. Yet in the UAE, Saudi, Oman and Kuwait, breaking any traffic laws will result in heavy fines.

Sonya, a corporate etiquette trainer and image consultant, describes it well: 'When I first moved to Lebanon from London, I was shocked by the lack of discipline on the road. I was perplexed by the self-made Lebanese driving rules which other drivers in the city understood, but which I could not seem to grasp. In fact, I took up yoga classes to help me deal with the stress of driving on Beirut's streets.'

It does appear as though drivers have some sort of secret language through which they communicate. Pedestrians running across a highway and taxis stopping suddenly to pick up a customer are common phenomena in many parts of the Arab world. Driving techniques are aggressive, and road accidents are, sadly, a frequent daily occurrence.

Traffic fatalities

For the world, fatalities from road crashes represented 2.1 per cent of fatalities from all causes. The highest percentage was in the United Arab Emirates (15.9 per cent) and the lowest in the Marshall Islands (0.3 per cent).

In the following ten countries, road crashes were responsible for the highest percentage of all fatalities: the United Arab Emirates, Qatar, Kuwait, Bahrain, Venezuela, Iran, Belize, Malaysia, Jordan and Mongolia.[7]

After living in Jordan for almost three years, Felix Bernhard seems to have made sense of the driving experience. 'In Germany, everybody follows the rules; the conflict starts when somebody does not follow the rules, then that one is basically the bad person. But here, no one is following the rules, therefore everybody is somehow always adjusting, always adjusting. People here do not drive against each other, they drive with each other. So you have to put yourself in a different state of mind.' Felix adds, 'What still annoys me is that people do not really reflect on how dangerous driving can be. I call it the *inshallah* lifestyle.'

---

7 A study published by the Transportation Research Institute at the University of Michigan, Ann Arbor, Michigan, February 2014.

The issue of road safety has become of increasing concern to civil societies and governments across the Arab world due to the high level of fatal accidents occurring every day. Campaigns have been promoting road safety and governments have been working to improve the conditions of roads and the enforcement of stricter regulations and penalties for offenders.

I would advise extreme caution when driving, and if you are visiting for short periods, then it would be better to either hire a driver or use a taxi and leave the driving to the skilled locals who are used to the driving conditions and are better trained to manoeuvre through the honking madness on the roads.

IF YOU ARE INVOLVED IN AN ACCIDENT

Even if it is a small bump and is clearly not your fault, you must stop, remain calm and call the police, your sponsor[8] (if it was a serious accident) and a trusted Arab friend. Avoid getting into an argument with the other driver. Do not be alarmed if you get a crowd of onlookers who will want to know what happened; the best thing you can do as a guest in that country is to stay calm, be polite and behave quietly. Shouting and aggressive behaviour will not help your case at all.

Wait for the police to arrive at the scene – it will take time, but you must have a police report for the insurance company in order to get your vehicle repaired. You will be asked to sign the police report, which will be written in Arabic. It is therefore

---

8   If you work in the Gulf countries, as a foreigner you will have a local who is sponsoring your visa and work permit.

advisable that you call a trusted Arab friend or colleague who can make sure that your statement was accurately translated.

There is zero tolerance for drinking and driving across the Arab world – an offence punishable by heavy fines and imprisonment. The offence is naturally greater in the countries where alcohol is banned and can lead to a jail sentence or deportation.

Driving in all sorts of weather

Sandstorms (known as *touz* in Arabic) sweep across Kuwait, Saudi and the UAE, turning everything orange and drastically restricting visibility on the road. In Jordan similar sandstorms are called '*khamasini* winds'.

Rare **rainfall** in the Gulf countries causes instant flooding and chaos for drivers.

Occasional **snowfall** in the Levant countries can leave some roads impassable.

Thick **fog** (usually in the morning) on the coast of the Arabian Gulf has been the cause of many fatal road accidents – especially on the highway between Dubai and Abu Dhabi.

TAXIS AND BUSES

Public transportation systems and their reliability vary across the Arab world, but taxis are widely available and are safe to use. Still, it is always better to check with someone local about the specifics of the area you are in.

When Chen Yi Xuan first came to this region, she thought that it was totally acceptable for her to sit in the front seat next to the driver in a taxi the way she would in China. She surprised a couple of taxi drivers until an Arab colleague explained to her that as a woman she had to sit in the back seat of the taxi, but a man would have the choice of either sitting in the front or the back.

Almost all of the Arab capital cities are not really walking cities. Although there are areas where you can walk, people use their cars or public transportation to go anywhere. Alexis McGinness found this surprising: 'The weather in Jordan is so beautiful yet I hardly see people walking on the streets. I love walking in cities because you discover so much more than when you are in a car. But the sidewalks here seem to be reserved for trees and stray cats.'

HOSPITALITY

Hospitality is an Arab and Muslim tradition deeply ingrained in the culture. Visitors are treated as kings and must always be fed and looked after. A Bedouin tradition actually stipulates that someone is allowed to stay in your home for three days before you can question why they are staying and when they will leave. So invitations to a home are a great honour that you should not turn down.

Within the first few months of her arrival to Jordan, Giovanna Negretti was overwhelmed with the warmth and generosity with which she was received by her hosts. 'Once you scratch the surface, the people here are incredibly loving and generous. I have never felt so at home as when I go on Fridays to my friend Salma's house and the whole family is there – her mother-in-law, sisters, brothers and children, and we spend the whole day just eating and sitting around chatting while our children are playing. They make us feel like we are family. And I really love how close friends and family can just drop by unannounced – this is so similar to my Latino culture – like the Arabs, we don't need to schedule a visit, family and friends are welcomed with a big smile and are always fed.'

Jonghee Son found Arab hospitality unlike anywhere else in the world: 'We would sometimes visit villages where people are really very poor, but still when we enter they would offer us food, anything, whatever little they have. When I worked as a journalist we visited the Syrian refugee camps; these people barely had enough for themselves, still they would offer us whatever they had. I have never seen this anywhere else in the world. It is so important for them to take care of the guest. I hope people here never lose this quality.'

While in Egypt, Jordan and the rest of the Levant you would likely get an invitation to someone's home for a meal, or at least a cup of coffee or mint tea, quite early on in the relationship, it is different in the Arabian Gulf countries. Although Gulf nationals would entertain you in restaurants, it takes quite some time to be invited into their homes.

Tari Lang remembers the first time she was invited to a senior Emirati's home when she was working in the UAE. 'We had been working together for almost three years when he invited me and my husband for a meal at his home during Ramadan. But I found a different experience in Jordan, where people I worked with invited me much more quickly into their homes. Still, everybody socialises in restaurants, so the social life is quite vibrant.'

Eric, too, has enjoyed this hospitality in some of the Gulf countries: 'What I really found incredibly enjoyable is when you get to a point where you know someone and you get to be invited into their home. It is very rare to be invited into some-one's home in the Gulf. That is very special and you know that you have gotten to know someone really well and it gives you an even better appreciation of who they are and how they live. I have really enjoyed that.'

Tony Goldner found that no matter where he went, the values of respect and dignity – which are central to Arab culture – were extended in the same way to guests and visitors from other cultures. In their experience, both Tony and Dan Monaghan have found that among the Gulf countries, the Kuwaitis tend to be more interested in socialising with foreigners and are more willing to open up about their lives in comparison to their neighbours in Saudi, the Emirates or Qatar, for exam-ple. In a short period of time, Dan was able to make a lot of Kuwaiti friends: 'I was invited into my Kuwaiti friends' homes regularly. And it was more so that they would invite me to their house than out to a restaurant. I always felt very welcomed. It was of course an all-male social group; I would never meet the wife or the daughters. The males have their section of the house where they entertain and that is where we would stay. We never mixed with the rest of the family. That is just not done here.'

Having lived in the region for some time, Peter Millett too understood the importance of hospitality for his Arab hosts: 'A British minister was visiting and the programme included an event at which our minister, along with the Jordanian min-ister and the mayor of the region we were in, would open a venue. We were going to go in and spend half an hour, a couple of speeches, cut a ribbon and leave. And it was about twelve o'clock. I had made the mistake of not looking carefully at the programme beforehand. On our way up I said to our visitors: They are going to offer us a *mansaf*[9] lunch and we are not going to be able to get away in time for our next event. Our British visiting delegation were more anxious about sticking to the schedule – used to lunch being a quick sandwich eaten in the car – but I told them that there was no way, we cannot not go to the lunch. It would have been upsetting for our hosts. It would have probably been okay on the day, but it would have left a bad taste. So it was better that we were late for our next appointment than upsetting the people who were hosting us.'

Giovanna received quite a special introduction to Jordanian hospitality: 'My mother-in-law had sent us a package, so I went to the main post office in downtown to collect it. I went to the offices upstairs and there were ten or twelve men in uniform (which looked a bit military to me) all standing around a desk, their backs towards me, and they were huddled there. I had on a sleeveless shirt because it was really hot and I was heavily pregnant. I went in and I said the only word I knew then which is *marhaba* (hello). One of the men turns around and looks me up and down and pokes the guy next to him; both of them look at me and I am starting to panic; is it my sleeveless shirt? Did I insult someone? Are they going to tell me to leave? I was really nervous. Then one of the men comes to me and hands me a spoon. And he says *yalla, yalla*[10], and ushers me towards the table and it turns out they were all

---

9   See 'Appendix: The most popular dishes in the Arab world', page 213

10   Arabic word meaning 'come on'.

eating *kunafeh*[11] and they wanted me to join them. And there I was, I had never seen *kunafeh* before in my life, and they kept saying *yalla, yalla*, because they wanted me to eat with them. That was amazing.'

It is important to strike a balance between your own culture and your host's. But more importantly – be genuine, be authentic. Like some other cultures, the Arabs are very observant and have a keen sense of what is a fake act and what is real. The effort that you make will be respected and highly appreciated.

When invited into an Arab's home, make sure you are dressed well – a very casual look may send the wrong message to your host. You should never go to someone's home for the first time empty-handed – take a small gift with you[12] – a box of chocolates or sweets; flowers are also appropriate for a hostess; and a small gift, such as sweets, for the children is a nice added touch. Avoid bringing a bottle of wine or any other alcohol – especially in the more conservative Gulf countries. A bottle of wine would be acceptable in the Levant – only if you are absolutely certain that your host drinks in public.[13]

In some societies you may be asked to remove your shoes before entering the house. Jonghee Son found this similar to her Korean culture: 'For Koreans it is very impolite for us to wear shoes in the house. But here it is different, you can wear shoes in a lot of homes here.'

---

11 An Arabic dessert dish famous in the Levant.

12 See also 'Gifts', page 186.

13 See box on 'Drinking alcohol', page 174.

FOOD AND GUESTS

Food is central to Arab hospitality, and the guest must be served generously. Dan found there was some similarities here with his Irish side of the family: 'Whenever I was invited to an Arab's home, depending on the time of day, I was always offered some sort of food. But no matter how full I was, I still had to eat. Not eating was simply not acceptable to my hosts.'

In the Arab world, lunch is the main meal of the day and is usually served around 2 p.m. Dinner varies among different societies – if there are no guests, some families prefer to have a light meal in the evening, while others prefer a hot cooked meal. Traditionally the family gathered around the table for lunch every day; however, these days, with the different working hours and school times, this has become more difficult, and so the Friday[14] family lunch has become even more important.

If you are invited to a meal in someone's home, there is often a great deal of socialising and small talk before the meal, with the food usually served late, and the evening comes to an end fairly quickly after the meal. It took Tony and his wife a while to get used to that: 'In the beginning we couldn't understand why we weren't being fed, and then we couldn't understand why nobody sat around afterwards to digest and talk. We later learned that food, in the sequence of events, is very different here. The activities and the socialising is done before eating, and dinner is not served till ten-thirty or eleven, which is really hard for an Australian stomach that is used to eating at seven-thirty.'

---

14   The weekend in the Arab world.

Wait to be told where to sit at the table, and be prepared that in some countries in the Gulf, the meal may be served on the floor. In that case, sit cross-legged or on one knee and make sure that you do not allow your feet to touch the cloth on which the food is laid.

The guest is honoured by sitting on the right hand of the host or across from him at the head of the table. Hospitality and generosity dictate that the guest is served with abundance. The host will closely look after the guest and frequently ask if there is anything that he needs. The guest is offered the most prized and delicious pieces of the meal, so do not decline what is offered to you, even if you don't think it looks very appetising. When you are full, you can leave a little bit of food on your plate, otherwise chances are that it will be filled again with more food. Avoid sensitive topics of conversation such as politics and religion and do not discuss business at the table unless your host decides to do so.

> ## Eating meat
> The level of consumption of animal protein depends almost entirely on wealth (and is itself a sign of wealth). Well-to-do households eat animal protein (beef, lamb, poultry, or fish) every day. Less affluent families eat animal protein once a week or even once a month.
>
> Although most Arab dishes include some sort of animal protein, legumes and vegetable dishes are also popular – especially in Jordan, Syria, Lebanon, Egypt and the Arab Maghreb countries. Vegetarians will find plenty of options.

Sally Zhang, a businesswoman from China, was overwhelmed by her hosts' hospitality: 'My customers in Egypt treat me like family; they invite me to their home and they cook for me

Sahtain

Sahtain is a word that you will hear used often around a meal. It literally means double health. It is said before, during and after a meal.

and give me the best pieces of meat and I always leave feeling stuffed with too much food.'

Meals are generally served family-style with the large serving dishes placed in the centre. Guests are always served first, followed by the eldest, and the youngest are served last. The host would first make sure that all his guests have filled their plates before he is served. Make it a point to comment on your host's generous hospitality and thank him throughout the meal, also complimenting the food as you eat – don't wait until the end.

In some countries, and especially in the tribal communities, the national dish is eaten without the use of cutlery. This has its own etiquette; the food is served on a large round platter placed in the middle, communal style, with guests sitting or standing around the main dish. You are first required to wash your hands, roll up the sleeve of your right arm and eat with your right hand using only the thumb and the first two fingers. You can use your left hand to help

Unfamiliar delicacies

Lamb is the most used meat across the Arab world and is sometimes served whole with the head attached. The sheep's tongue, brains and even intestines are considered a delicacy in most Arab countries – especially in the Bedouin communities. These are cooked using a number of spices and can be quite delicious. As a foreigner you will rarely encounter these dishes, but if your host offers you the prized sheep's tongue, it is best not to decline it.

you cut the meat. Your fingers are not supposed to touch your mouth and you are meant to eat only from the small area in the dish right in front of you.

Toshihiro Abe found the experience very different from his own expectations: 'It's true that in the Emirates they have lots of money and they drive very nice cars, but when I was invited to an Emirate's home it was really nice and simple; we sat on the floor and the food was served on the floor, we ate by hand all together from the main dish. It was a beautiful experience, and I felt very welcomed.'

Since rice is the main staple in most of the national dishes, it is also common for Arabs to eat using a tablespoon instead of a fork and knife. In that case you should also use your right hand for eating. If the table is set Western style, you can use the fork and knife in the regular European way.

When he first came to the region, Peter Millett was not prepared for the formal, social lunch events: 'Sitting down, gentle talk, standing round the *mansaf*. The top people at the top table and everybody on other tables. Having people take the best bits of meat and giving it to me. And trying to do it so I didn't have too much to eat, going to wash my hands and then sitting down for the *kunafeh*[15] and the tea and coffee. I've got used to it now, but that first time, I wasn't prepared for it, it was the social protocols that are so important. I adapted and picked up the signals, following their lead. And people are

---

15   A traditional Arabic dessert dish very popular in Jordan, Palestine, Syria and Lebanon. It is made of a kind of white cheese covered with a special kind of string pastry. It is served hot with syrup.

patient here, as long as you are showing respect, giving the honour and the dignity which they are looking for, then they can be patient with your mistakes.'

Flatbread (known as pita bread in the West) is an important staple in Arabic cuisine. Many dishes, especially in the Lebanese and Syrian cuisine, are eaten with bread. The mezze is a wide variety of small dishes that are placed in the middle of the table and shared communally. Here you take a small piece of the bread and use it to eat directly out of the mezze dishes.

Alexis McGinness enjoyed trying the different flavours and particularly the late breakfast they would sometimes get delivered to the office: 'I had no idea that falafel is a breakfast item; in the US we have it for dinner, but it's nothing like the real thing you get here.' Chen Yi Xuan was a bit disappointed that Arabic food is not as spicy as most Chinese food she is used to, but she loves kebab and Arabic desserts, especially *kunafeh*.

An Arab's table is lavish with plenty of food – something which many Westerners think is unnecessary wastefulness. However, rest assured that none of the food gets thrown away, whether at official public events or in people's homes. A host will make certain that all support staff – servants, drivers, security people – are fed, and any food left over is given to charity.

That is why Arabs are sometimes surprised when they are invited to a foreigner's home and only one or two main dishes are served. An Arab would like to be received with the same level of generosity he is accustomed to giving his own guests.

You should also offer your Arab guest a second helping at least three times, as most Arabs are taught that it would be impolite to accept food the first time.

Dan Monaghan notes the cultural difference in this aspect: 'In the UK, for example, if you go to someone's house and they offer you food and you say, "No thank you, I'm not hungry," they will not give you food. It's simple, straightforward.' Dan recalls an experience that one of his Arab friends shared with him: 'My Arab friend, who was living in Australia at the time, was invited to his friend's home there. When they offered him food, of course being brought up to be very polite, he would say, "Thank you, I'm fine," even though he would be genuinely hungry, so they would say, "Okay," and would not offer him any food and he would leave very hungry.'

Halal is an Arabic word that means permissible by God. *Halal*, in connection with food, means food that Muslims are permitted to consume under Islamic Sharia law. The opposite is *haram*, which means prohibited by God. *Halal* and *haram* are universal terms that apply to all facets of life. In relation to food, pork and alcohol are considered *haram* and are therefore forbidden for all Muslims. *Halal* here also refers to the proper Islamic way for slaughtering animals before they can be cooked and eaten.

Pork products

In some Arab countries where there is a large expat community or a large Arab Christian minority, you will find that pork products are sold in some of the large supermarkets. But these would be very clearly marked and in areas that are isolated from the rest of the products. If you are entertaining a Muslim at your house, make sure you do not have any pork products on the table.

Drinking alcohol

The consumption, importation, brewing of, and trafficking in liquor is strictly against the law in Kuwait, Saudi Arabia, Sudan, Yemen and Sharjah (one of the emirates in the UAE). Restrictions exist in the rest of the Gulf countries where alcohol is served in hotels and some restaurants, but in some cases a special permit is required to purchase and consume alcohol in your home. Alcohol is legal in the rest of the Arab countries not mentioned above and is sold in regular liquor stores.

Although many Muslim Arabs may drink alcohol when they travel abroad, they will not drink in their homes or at official functions.

COFFEE AND TEA

There are several legendary accounts of how coffee came to be a drink, but the common belief is that human consumption of coffee dates as far back as the sixth-century Abyssinia (modern-day Ethiopia). The fruit of the plant, known as coffee cherries, were eaten as a food rather than a beverage. By the ninth century, coffee trees were being cultivated in Yemen and used by the Sufis[16] to keep themselves alert during their late-night prayers and religious rituals.

In an attempt to prevent its cultivation elsewhere, the Arabs imposed a ban on the export of fertile coffee beans, a restriction that was eventually circumvented in 1616 by the Dutch, who brought live coffee plants back to the Netherlands to be grown in greenhouses.[17] Coffee eventually spread throughout

---

16   Sufism is mystical Islamic belief and practice in which Muslims seek to find the truth of divine love and knowledge through direct personal experience of God.

17   International Coffee Organisation website (ico.org).

the world and found its place as an intellectual, stimulating, and often subversive agent that carried with it a lot of cultural significance.

The traditional **Arabic coffee** (*qahwa*) – a light gold-coloured liquid – is flavour-rich with cardamom, and other spices like saffron, cloves, and sometimes cinnamon. This traditional method uses coffee beans that are not roasted, so it is a beverage entirely unlike what most people think of as coffee.

Some establishments and offices have a dedicated man to serve the traditional Arabic coffee, who is known as the *qahwaji*. This coffee is served from a special pot called a *dalleh*, which the server holds in his left hand while he offers the coffee cups in his right hand. The cups are small and without a handle, and the portion of coffee served is tiny – about three or four sips.

You should take the cup in your right hand and do not put it down in between sips. Once you have finished, you hand your empty cup back to the server. If you do not wish to have any more, then gently shake your cup from side to side to indicate that you are done. Otherwise the server will keep refilling your cup with more coffee.

Arabic coffee is served as a sign of hospitality, friendship and agreement. At a *Jaha*[18], for example, a cup of coffee is placed in front of the leader of the tribe that is coming with a request – either to resolve a big disagreement, ask for forgiveness for a wrong, or to ask for a girl's hand in marriage for one of their sons – tribal traditions dictate that the tribe leader will not

18 See 'What is a *Jaha*?', page 36.

drink the coffee served to him until his request is met.

Arabic coffee is served at happy occasions but also at solemn ones. Expect to be served this coffee, in addition to a cup of tea, at every meeting you go to. It is best not to decline this, regardless of how much coffee and tea you have already consumed elsewhere that day; you don't have to finish your cup, a couple of sips will suffice.

Turkish coffee (also known as Greek or Armenian coffee in other countries) is prepared with finely powdered roast coffee beans boiled in a special pot, with sugar according to taste, before being served in a small cup where the sediment settles. When offered this kind of coffee you will be asked if you would like it: *sada* – without sugar, *wasat* – with medium sugar, or *sukkar ziyadeh* – extra sweet.

Tea customs began in the Middle East when Morocco became an importer of black tea in the eighteenth century. However, the Moroccans then started importing green tea, which became a major part of their culture. The famous Moroccan tea is made from gunpowder green tea with spearmint leaves and sugar; occasionally lemon verbena is also added to give it a distinct lemony flavour.

Tea is an important part of daily life across the Middle East. Black tea boiled with fresh mint leaves, sweetened, and sometimes with milk added, is served with breakfast, after the main lunch meal and after dinner. It is usually served in a small glass cup known as *istikana*. In some countries in the Gulf, they infuse their tea with fresh cardamom or sage instead of mint leaves.

AL MAJLIS/DIWANIYA/DIWAN

Al majlis is an Arabic term meaning 'a place of sitting'. It can refer to a 'council', to describe a group or special gathering for a common purpose – be it social, administrative or religious. It also refers to the legislature and is part of the name given to the council, assembly or parliament. For example, *Majlis al nuwwab* is the House of Representatives.

In a social setting, the *majlis* is a private place (similar to a large sitting room) where guests are received, entertained and served freshly brewed Arabic coffee and mint tea. The floors are covered with Persian carpets, and guests sit on cushions placed against the walls either directly on the floor or on a raised shelf.

Today this social tradition of the *majlis* continues, particularly in the Gulf countries, where wealthy families build a separate hall that is secluded from other parts of the house to serve as a *majlis*, or *diwaniya*, as it is known in Kuwait, or *diwan* as it is known in the Levant.

The *majlis* or *diwaniya* has preserved its important place in the social, political and economic life of the Arab Gulf countries in particular. It is the place where men gather to discuss business and politics and sometimes poetry and literature. It is a place where decisions are cooked, deals are struck and opinions exchanged. Similar to a political salon or a social club, *al majlis* or the *diwaniya* has remained exclusively for men. However, very recently, women were allowed to attend some *diwaniyas* in Kuwait and Doha.

Incense

Bakhoor or *bukhoor* is the Arabic word given to a particular incense: scented bricks or wood chips that are soaked in fragrant essential oils and mixed with other natural ingredients such as resin, musk and sandalwood. *Oudh* (the Arabic name for agarwood) is the most popular.

Bukhoor is burnt in a traditional incense burner called a *mabkhara*. Its fragrant thick smoke is used to perfume the house and clothing and boost positive energy and dismiss bad spirits. It is also used at special occasions such as weddings, and is commonly passed amongst guests in the *majlis* as a gesture of hospitality. A guest would gently move his right hand above the *mabkhara* whiffing the fragrant smoke towards himself.

CAFÉS AND RESTAURANTS

Social entertaining outside the home is quite active across most of the Arab world, with a wide variety of very high-quality restaurants serving international cuisine ranging from Italian, French and North American to Chinese, Japanese and Asian fusion. International cafés and traditional coffeehouses are also very popular in cities and towns across the Arab world.

Socialising with the opposite sex

In the countries of the Levant as well as in Egypt and the Arab North African countries, it is normal and acceptable for the sexes to mix publicly in restaurants and cafés. However, this is not the case for Gulf nationals in their countries, where unmarried couples or friends would not feel comfortable socialising in public places. Many restaurants are divided into sections for 'families' and another for men on their own. So it is common to see tables with groups of men out on their own and separate tables with groups of women on their own.

The social rules for non-Arabs are more lax, but you must never forget the overall conservative nature of Arab culture, which varies in strictness from one country to the other.

The coffee-house culture in the Arab world has its roots in the sixteenth century, when drinking coffee outside the house was encouraged first in Yemen and then across the Arabian peninsula. Today it is a thriving culture where people gather to socialise, discuss the political issues of the day, gossip, play backgammon or chess and smoke *argeeleh*.[19] The traditional coffee houses were exclusively for men. Today, there are many more modern coffee houses and cafés that cater for both men and women – in addition to all the international franchises such as Starbucks, Costa and Caribou.

Smoking the *argeeleh*

An *argeeleh* or *shisha* (or water-pipe) is a single or multi-stemmed instrument for smoking flavoured tobacco, in which the smoke passes through a glass water basin before it is inhaled through a long plastic tube. It is believed to have originated in Persia and spread to Egypt and the Levant during the rule of the Ottoman Empire.

Today the *argeeleh* is an ever-present part of the Arab coffee-house (and some restaurants) social culture and is smoked by both men and women. You will find people who do not smoke cigarettes or cigars but do smoke the *argeeleh*. People enjoy it more for the social habit rather than the actual tobacco. It's an excuse to gather with friends to chat and bond.

---

19   The waterpipe or *hookah*. Also known as *nargeeleh* or *shisha*.

Nightlife is quite vibrant in the Arab countries where alcohol is permitted. Beirut, Cairo and Dubai are the Arab capitals most famous for their lively cosmopolitan nightlife – European-style bars, clubs and lounges, where a mixture of Arabic and Western pop music is played and people enjoy a meal and a drink. While in Dubai (and all the other Gulf cities) you will rarely find any locals in these places, elsewhere in the Arab world, the locals do enjoy a good night out – especially on a Thursday night (the equivalent of Friday night in the West.)

Even though she has been in the region for a relatively short time, Alexis McGinness enjoys the social life here with her Arab friends: 'Every time I have gone out with them and I am the only American, they would speak in English to make me feel more comfortable, or if they do speak in Arabic, someone will fill me in and I can follow the conversation by the facial expressions and the body gestures. I always feel very welcomed. They really make an effort to reach

Qat-chewing in Yemen

Qat or *khat* is a slow-growing shrub or tree found in the Horn of Africa and the Arabian peninsula. *Qat* is a mild narcotic that is very popular in Yemen. Yemenis chew the leaves and store a wad in one cheek as the *qat* slowly breaks down into the saliva and enters the bloodstream. Since chewing the leaves is not forbidden in Islam, evening *qat* ceremonies and regular salon gatherings (men and women separately) to chew and chat about matters great and small are regular forms of socialising in Yemen. It is believed that the leaf has energy-boosting qualities and numbs hunger.

All kinds of narcotics are illegal across the Arab world; possession and use of any kind of drugs is a very serious offence.

out.' Alexis found the social nightlife here a bit different from what she is used to in the US: 'When we go out dancing, there isn't a dance floor. Everyone dances next to their table and they only interact with the people they came with. Maybe it goes back to the family relations, but here I found that unless you are formally introduced to somebody, you wouldn't just go up and talk to them.'

Smoking

Non-smokers may find socialising in public places in the Arab world a bit of a challenge. While some restaurants do have a non-smoking section (which in reality is not very effective); restaurants where smoking is prohibited are very rare.

Smoking is against the law in all airports and most government buildings. But in some Arab countries that law is not strictly adhered to.

Arabs are known for their generosity and hospitality, which leads to an interesting dynamic when the time comes to pay the bill at a restaurant or café. The concept of splitting the bill in the Arab world is not really accepted (unless it is a group of friends who regularly go out together).

Dan Monaghan found this aspect quite stressful: 'The first thing that I found unusual here is the concept of an invitation to a restaurant. In the UK if someone says I am inviting you, an invitation would be to their home or a special event somewhere, whereas here, people regularly invite you to a restaurant and pay for the entire meal. That was a bit strange to me.

'But the more I went out socially with my Arab friends, I found I was getting more stressed about the issue of paying the bill. I would be driving to a restaurant and I would have this apprehension – the bill is going to come, I want to pay, but then we all get into this whole debate and fight over the bill and the winner is the one who is able to snatch the bill and pay first. And I am always conscious of appearing to be miserly and not fighting hard enough to pay the bill. So I have learned that now I make the point that when we get to the coffee, I get up quietly to go to the bathroom and I go and pay the bill and go back to the table and continue the evening. For me that whole concept was just totally alien.'

Tony Goldner says that this is a classic issue that he, too, has often faced: 'I have had to take to ploys like going to the bathroom fifteen minutes before the end of the meal to find the waiter and give him my credit card to pay, because the Arab would do that and you have to find a way to do it first. That is very deeply cultural behaviour related to the importance of generosity and hospitality in this culture.'

Dan noted another social tradition that he liked: 'Now that we have been living in Dubai for a few years, we have a lot of Arab friends with whom we

Tipping

Bakhsheesh is the Arabic colloquial word for tipping. It is customary to tip anyone who does a service for you – from the boy who helps you carry your groceries, to the attendant at the petrol station, and of course waiters at restaurants and cafés. There isn't a set percentage tip that is expected at restaurants, as it is usually left to the customer's discretion. However, check the bill, and if a service charge is included then you can leave a small additional amount (either 5 or 10 per cent or just rounding it up); but if there isn't an added service charge, then a 15 per cent tip would be appropriate. When in doubt, ask someone local for specific guidance.

socialise regularly. When we go out as a group with our Arab friends – some are married couples and some are single – if there are any single girls with us, they are never expected to pay any money towards the bill – the whole bill is split among the men only. I like that.'

DOGS AND PETS

The Quran instructs Muslims not to abuse animals and to treat them with compassion, and states that all creation praises God in its own way. There are several stories of the Prophet Mohammed telling his companions of the virtue of saving the life of a dog by quenching its thirst. However, the majority of Muslim scholars consider dogs to be ritually unclean and would consequently not come into contact with a dog. Therefore, if you have a dog in your home and you are entertaining an Arab guest, I would advise you to keep your dog in another room to avoid any discomfort to your guest. Having said that, you will find a lot of Arabs who do not consider dogs to be unclean and do keep them as pets in their homes. Most of the Arab cities have an animal hospital or clinic and if you ask your local mentor, someone would be able to recommend a local vet for your pet.

An insult
The word for dog in Arabic is *kalb* and can be used as an insult or swear word. A variation on the insult is to say, '*Ibn al kalb*' – meaning son of a dog.

You will find a lot of stray cats on the streets of many cities and towns across the Arab world. Many people feed the cats that wander into their gardens but few would allow them inside their homes.

WEDDINGS

Weddings are elaborate celebrations that can last for several weeks and involve the entire extended family, friends and acquaintances. Each region has its own local specific traditions, but the wedding remains a major event across the Arab world, with all the celebrations – dinners, lunches and parties – taking place before the actual wedding day.

In the Gulf countries and among traditional Muslims, wedding parties are segregated, and the main celebration is attended by women only. The bride wears a white dress and the groom either wears the traditional *dishdash* (*thoub*) and *abaya*[20] or a Western-style suit and tie. The celebration almost always involves a lavish dinner, loud music and dancing that goes on well past midnight.[21] Weddings are the occasions where people go all-out and the women – especially if they are close relatives of the bride and groom – dress up in their finest evening clothes and jewellery.

Dan Monaghan recalls the time he attended a traditional Kuwaiti wedding: 'We came to the front of the male area of the house. All the male relatives were lined up wearing their traditional clothes. We walked in, shook hands with the men in the receiving line; we were then offered Arabic coffee, tea, dates and chocolates, and then we walked out of the other door to the car. The whole thing took no more than ten minutes. That was a strange experience for me, but I then learned that the big party with all the dancing

---

20   See 'Appearance and dress codes', page 156.

21   An Arab Christian wedding would start with the church service in the afternoon, followed by an evening reception or dinner and dance party.

and the lavish buffet was held in another location for the women only.'

The *zaffeh*

The *zaffeh* – a predominantly Middle Eastern tradition – started off as a procession of dancers with drums, bagpipes, horns and swords that accompanied the groom and his male family members to the bride's house. The aim was to be as grandiose as they could while making as much noise as possible. The purpose of the *zaffeh* was to let people know that a wedding was going to take place – since marriages were also subject to the community's approval as well as the family's.

Today the tradition of the *zaffeh* has been adapted and modified but still continues to be an important part of any wedding, and a very elaborate and orchestrated entrance for the bride and groom. Each country has its own style of *zaffeh*, using different musical instruments, songs and chanting.

When he later attended a mixed wedding in Jordan, Dan found it a completely different experience: 'The *zaffeh* was something I had never experienced before, but it gave such an amazing atmosphere in the house, with the ululations, and the big sword to cut the wedding cake. For me it was very noisy and very colourful, but it was a beautiful, happy, grand celebration. I felt lucky to be a part of it.'[22]

The bridal henna night remains a very important custom in many Arab and Muslim countries.[23] Held a few days before the wedding night and attended by women only, it's when the

---

22   See also 'Music', page 200; and 'Dance', page 203.

23   Jews, Sikhs and Hindus also traditionally celebrate the henna night.

Ululation

Ululation (the high-pitched, loud vibrating sound made by the rapid movement of the tongue, uvula and hand) is used by women across the Arab world to express joy at celebrations – especially weddings. In the Arab world you may also hear women ululating at the funeral of a martyr, as Muslims believe that martyrs are blessed and go directly to Paradise.

bride is adorned with intricate henna designs on her hands and feet. In Algeria, the bride's mother-in-law traditionally paints the henna on the bride's hands, while in other Arab countries the bride's female relatives apply the henna on her hands – but they have to be happily married, otherwise they might bring bad luck to the bride.

Henna

Henna is the dye prepared from the plant of the same name, and has been used since ancient times to dye skin, hair and finger-nails, as well as fabrics and leather.[24] Henna is believed to have blessings and is applied for luck as well as beauty.

GIFTS

In line with their hospitable and generous nature, Arabs like to give gifts to honour their guests. The nature and value of such gifts differ from country to country and also depend on the person doing the giving. This is considered standard behaviour and should not be misinterpreted as a form of bribery. A lot of foreign companies have strict rules against accepting

---

24 Muslim men may use henna as a dye for their hair and their beards – this is considered a commendable tradition of the Prophet Mohammed – hence the dark orange colour of the beards of some of the Muslim clerics in Saudi Arabia and Yemen.

any gifts; my advice would be to assess the situation carefully. Turning down a gift can cause a lot of offence and irreparable damage to the relationship.

In the same spirit, an Arab appreciates receiving a thoughtful gift; however, do not feel you are obliged to do so, especially in the early stages of the relationship. Some business people carry with them a variety of company branded items such as USBs or diaries. These are appropriate gifts, but be careful not to leave behind something that could be considered cheap or shabby.

When presenting a gift, do so with both hands and do not expect it to be opened when it is received. Avoid taking a bottle of wine or any alcohol as a host or hostess gift – unless you know the person very well and you are certain that he is comfortable with alcohol.[25] If you are being received by both the man and his wife, then flowers for the hostess would be an appropriate gift. Chocolate, sweets or biscuits/cookies – especially if they are something special from your own country – would make a very thoughtful gift for such an occasion. Avoid any personal gifts for the wife (such as perfume, jewellery or any items of clothing); however, something for the children would be highly appreciated.

As for wedding gifts, traditions vary among countries and families and tribes within the same country. In the more modern Arab capitals, they now have a gift registry included in the invitation card. If you are close to the person who invited you, then you can choose a gift on the registry and have it delivered to either the bride's or groom's parents' home before the

---

25   See box on 'Drinking alcohol', page 174.

wedding. Alternatively, you can send a flower arrangement to their home or to the venue of the wedding party. (Don't forget to include a card with a message of best wishes and your name.) In some regions, wedding guests are expected to give gifts in the form of cash placed in a sealed envelope – meant to help the newlyweds start their new life together.

To avoid any embarrassment, in these specific situations it is best to ask someone local about the traditions of that particular family or tribe and what they would expect from their guests.

FUNERALS
Muslims are instructed to bury their dead as soon as possible after the death occurs, preferably within hours. The actual funeral prayers are held in a mosque, after which the shrouded body is buried in the ground without a casket. Grave markers are simple, because outwardly lavish displays are discouraged in Islam. In Saudi Arabia in particular, graves are sometimes unmarked or marked only with a simple wreath.

Women are discouraged from attending Muslim funerals, and as a foreigner you are not expected to attend a funeral, but you are expected to pay your respects and give condolences to the family of the deceased during the three-day mourning period known in Arabic as *aza*.

Arab Christians also bury their dead soon after the death occurs. There are no public funeral homes in the Arab world and, unlike some Western traditions, the deceased does not lie in an open casket for visitors to bid him farewell. The funeral service is held in church and only very close family members go to the actual burial site. Other people pay their respects to the family during the *aza*, which is held either in the family home or in a public hall.

Condolences are also segregated. Usually mornings of the *aza* are for the women to visit, and the afternoons and evenings are for the men. At a Muslim *aza*, a cleric would be reciting verses from the Quran while people enter the room, shake hands with members of the bereaved family, then take a seat. Bitter Arabic coffee is served, along with some plain dates, and visitors are not expected to stay for more than fifteen to twenty-five minutes. Women remove make-up and jewellery and wear black, sometimes with a white scarf or white blouse if the deceased is not a very close relative. Men wear dark suits and ties or their national *thoub* and *shmakh*.[26]

'One of the first condolences I went to was for a high-ranking official who had lost his son in an accident.' Peter Millett recalls the event: 'There were hundreds and hundreds of people and the man was clearly shocked out of his mind that he had lost his eldest son, yet he had to spend the next three days receiving all these people. In my mind, I thought this is terrible. This poor man should be left alone to mourn with his wife. But then after going to a few condolences, I began to realise that it is that very demonstration of respect, that everybody is condoling with you, and that overwhelming show of support and respect is a means of overcoming the grief. And that actually helps the family cope with the tragedy. That was a very good illustration of how my mindset had not understood what was actually happening.'

---

26   See 'Appearance and dress codes', page 156

Because of the very close social and family ties in the Arab world, many organisations have compassionate leave policies that allow people to attend an *aza*.

As a foreigner, this is one social duty that means a lot to your Arab hosts. If a death occurs in the family of someone you work closely with, make it a point to enquire about the arrangements for the *aza* and how you can visit to pay your respects within the first three days.

9

SPORT, MEDIA AND THE ARTS

SPORT

One of the main universal points of connection that transcends borders and cultures, sport is compulsory in all schools across the Arab world. Qatar has even gone as far as dedicating the second Tuesday of every February as a National Sports Day – a public holiday in which everyone, including all ministries and government departments, take part in some sort of sport activity.

The most popular sport across the Arab world is of course **football** (also known as soccer in the US). People in the Arab world closely follow the various leagues and championships including the Premier League and the Champion's League. Football fans here are very serious about their favourite teams such as Barcelona, Real Madrid, Manchester United and Arsenal.

Every country also has its own football federation and league. National teams compete in various regional championships such as the Arab Nations Cup – which has, unfortunately, not been held regularly due to political unrest.

Basketball is also popular, especially with the younger generation, and national teams compete in the Arab Nations Cup Basketball.

Camel racing continues to be a popular traditional sport in Saudi Arabia, Bahrain, Qatar, UAE, Oman, Jordan and even Egypt. Camels are often controlled by child jockeys, but allegations of human rights abuses have led to nationwide bans on underage jockeys. In 2002, the UAE was the first to ban the use of children under fifteen as jockeys in camel racing, and Qatar followed suit and imposed the ban in 2005. Now robotic jockeys are widely used instead.

Falconry remains an important part of the Arab heritage and culture and is considered one of the traditional sports in the Arabian Gulf countries. The UAE reportedly spends over $27 million annually towards the protection and conservation of wild falcons, and has set up several state-of-the-art falcon hospitals in Abu Dhabi and Dubai. The Abu Dhabi Falcon Hospital is the largest falcon hospital in the whole word. The saker falcon is the most traditional species and is flown against the houbara bustard, sand grouse, stone curlew, other birds and hares. There are several breeding farms in the Emirates, Qatar and Saudi Arabia and every year falcon beauty contests and demonstrations take place – the most important of which is the Abu Dhabi International Hunting and Equestrian Exhibition (ADIHEX) – the largest and only dedicated hunting, equestrian and outdoor sports exhibition in the region.

Horse racing. Known throughout the world for its incredible energy, intelligence and gentle disposition, the Arabian horse is the oldest known breed of riding horse and today is one of the most popular and sought-after breeds. Bred by the Bedouins in the harsh desert conditions, where food was scarce and war a regular occurrence, the Arabian horse became its owner's most treasured possession. The Bedouin would share his water, food and even his tent with his horse; as a result, the Arabian horse developed a close affinity to man and a high intelligence. During the frequent raids, the Arab relied on the speed and endurance of his mount for his survival. Mares were used for quick surprise attacks against enemies, as stallions could not be relied upon to remain quiet.

Over the centuries, the Bedouin tribes zealously maintained the purity of the breed. Today the purebred Arabian is virtually the same as that ridden in ancient Arabia and remains the undisputed champion of endurance events.

The Prophet Mohammed was instrumental in spreading the Arabian horse's influence around the world in the seventh century. He directed that horses should be bred by the faithful, so that they would be better prepared to go forth and spread the faith of Islam.[1]

Horse racing was a major sport and favourite pastime in pre-Islamic Arabia and was considered part of the essential military training, but also provided entertainment for people from all walks of life. And according to the *Encyclopaedia of Islam*: 'The Prophet did not forbid racing, which fostered rivalry between breeders and encouraged the preservation and increase of the stocks of horses so much reduced by the wars.'[2]

---

1 *Horse Racing in Islam*, Mumtaz Ali Tajddin S.Ali.

2 1965, 2:953.

The biggest horse race in the region is the Dubai World Cup –
which has a purse of $10 million – making it the largest purse
in the world. The race is held at the Meydan Racecourse in
Dubai, which is reported to be the world's largest track.

Gambling is illegal in the Arab world, so there is no betting
on horse races.

Motorsport is another popular activity in many of the Arab countries. It is an important part of Jordan's history, having been first introduced by King Hussein in the late fifties. The famous Jordan Rally was first held in 1981 and is now recognised as one of the leading events on the FIA Middle East Rally Championship. Car rallies are also held in Lebanon, Oman, Qatar and Kuwait.

Illegal street racing

Tafheet, also known as Arab or Saudi drifting, is illegal street racing, which is basically driving regular, non-modified cars at very high speeds (around 160–260 kph) across wide highways, drifting sideways and recovering by repeatedly using opposite lock steering. *Tafheet* events are mostly seen on the wide sectioned highways in Riyadh and other parts of Saudi. It is an illegal practice, as it has little to no concern for the safety of the drivers or the spectators.

Golf, an unlikely sport for the geography and terrain of the Middle East, is also becoming a popular game, with some world-famous courses in Abu Dhabi, Dubai, Bahrain and Qatar. The Dubai Desert Classic is one of the well-known international golf tournaments played here.

THE MEDIA

The media in the Arab world has been, and continues for the most part, to operate under the strong influence of the state authorities, although the level and directness of government control over the national print and broadcast media varies from one Arab country to the other. Traditionally, the media in Arab countries were regarded as the propaganda tools by which their regimes maintained their power and control. However, after the appearance of satellite television in the 1990s, things began to change and the new millennium saw an explosion in the number of new television, radio, print and online media – mostly privately owned, commercial ventures.

Historically, the countries that have had the strongest influence on pan-Arab media are Egypt and Saudi Arabia. As the most populous, and one of the most politically influential countries in the Arab world, Egypt has often been viewed as the Arab region's leader in media, politics and culture and has led the region in the development of a relatively open print and broadcast media. Saudi Arabia, through its incredible oil revenue, has had a strong influence on the major pan-Arab newspapers and satellite channels. The Lebanese, on the other hand – with their satellite TV networks – Future, LBC, Al Jadeed – have been very influential in setting trends in many areas of life across the Arab world.

A large number of the Arab media's problems today are structural. Years of state ownership, restrictive laws and regulatory measures coupled with self-censorship by the media itself have had a negative impact on the standard and level of professionalism in the Arab media in general.

> ### How free is the media?
>
> The continued political unrest in the region, compounded by the Syrian conflict and the rise of ISIS, have led the authorities in the Arab world to tighten their control on the media. The Freedom House *Freedom of the Press Report* for 2014 ranked the media of most of the Arab countries as 'not free' and only four Arab countries as 'partly free' – these are Lebanon, Tunisia, Algeria and Kuwait.

Satellite television in the 1990s brought dramatic changes to the Middle East. Satellite dishes cover the rooftops in most cities across the Arab world, even reaching some of the more remote places. The number of 'free to air' channels has exceeded six hundred – thereby creating some fierce competition among broadcasters, which are providing audiences across the Arab world with a wide variety of news channels, talk shows, sitcoms, music and movies. In addition to the Arab channels, a number of international networks broadcast Arabised channels, such as BBC Arabic, Sky News Arabia, France24 Arabic, CNBC Arabia and Russia Today Arabic.

THE INTERNET, MOBILE PHONES AND SOCIAL MEDIA

Internet connectivity has transformed the ways in which millions of people do business, learn, socialise and interact with government. Although Arab internet users today make up less than 0.5 per cent of the global internet population, they have been growing at a faster than average rate – in the range of 20 per cent annually.[3] Figures indicate that the internet penetra-

---

3   *The Arab World Online 2014: Trends in internet and mobile usage in the Arab region,*

tion rate in the Arab region as a whole stands at approximately 52 per cent.[4] While high-income countries in the Arab region have achieved relatively high levels of connectivity and penetration rates, most Arab countries are still lagging behind in terms of accessible broadband. According to an Arab online survey, accessibility and connectivity, cost and lack of content in Arabic were the top three challenges facing internet users in the region.

Although digital e-commerce penetration in the Middle East is lagging behind all other regions in the world, the economic impact of internet growth in the Arab region will undoubtedly increase going forward. It is estimated that in the year 2020, around 20 per cent of the labour market in the Middle East and North Africa region will be related to internet and technology industries.[5]

The Arab World Online 2014 survey

- 64 per cent of respondents have never purchased books online
- 54 per cent of respondents have never purchased airline tickets online
- 55 per cent of respondents don't purchase other items online
- The internet is the primary source of news for 35 per cent of respondents
- 28 per cent get their news from social media while another 30 per cent get it from traditional media sources

---

Mohammed bin Rashid School of Government.

4 Internet World Stats (internetworldstats.com), 2015 figures.

5 *Broadband Networks in the Middle East and North Africa: Accelerating High-Speed Internet Access*, The World Bank 2014.

Mobile phone penetration rates in the MENA region is at 124 per cent of the population and the mobile subscriber base is expected to grow further, overtaking Europe by 2016 as the second largest region for mobile subscribers.[6] This critical mass of internet and mobile users in the Arab region has opened a massive new market, as well as some ambitious service-delivery initiatives, such as smart government, mobile government, smart cities and technology-enabled citizen engagement initiatives.[7]

The MENA region already has the second largest social networking audience in the world.[8] The social media platforms most popular among Arabs are Facebook and Twitter, with LinkedIn and Instagram catching on more among the younger generation. In terms of Facebook penetration, Qatar leads in the Arab region, followed by the UAE, with Jordan, Lebanon, and Bahrain rounding out the top five countries.[9] Egypt continues to constitute about a quarter of all Facebook users in the region. The country with the highest number of Twitter users is Saudi Arabia, accounting for over 40 per cent of all active Twitter users in the Arab region.[10]

6 *Mobile Factbook*, January 2015.

7 *The Arab World Online 2014: Trends in internet and mobile usage in the Arab region*, Mohammed bin Rashid School of Government.

8 eMarketers.com

9 arabsocialmediareport.com

10 Ibid.

Arab attitudes to social media

Arab users believe social media serves as a 'life enhancer', brightening up one's day and adding excitement to their lives. For many young Arab individuals, being connected to social media makes them feel 'alive'. This description of social media is true throughout all the Arab regions, without any exception.[11]

FILM AND TELEVISION PRODUCTION

Known as the Hollywood of the Middle East, Egypt has long been the centre of modern media production in the Arabic-speaking world. Egyptian films and television dramas are avidly consumed not just in Egypt but all over the Arab world. They range from tacky melodramas to internationally acclaimed, award-winning films of high artistic value. In addition to its vast pools of talent in all fields of the film and television industry, Egypt has the third-largest production facilities in the world after the United States and India. After Egypt, Syria was, prior to 2012, the second country in the Arabic TV-series production field, followed by Kuwait – which targets solely the Gulf market.

Hollywood recognition

The Jordanian film *Theeb* was nominated for an Oscar in the best foreign-language film category in 2015.

In recent years, filmmakers and business executives from the United States, South Asia and Europe have shown a growing interest in this region, not only as a potential market but also as a wellspring of talent and inspiration. Morocco, Tunisia and Jordan have succeeded in establishing a track record with

11 Ibid.

the film industry in the West as excellent filming locations, with local talent providing all the support that is needed.

MUSIC

As with film and television production, Egypt – followed by Lebanon – has long dominated trends in music across the Arab world. As it gained its independence from decades of foreign rule, Egypt's nationalist movement brought with it its own style of music. Although quite alive and unique in many ways, Arabic music is the result of a long history of interaction, with many other regional styles of music mixed in with the varied tastes of the people that make up the Arab world today.

Instruments used in Arabic music are too diverse and too many to list. But the most commonly used are:[12]

The *oud*. Its name derives from the Arabic for 'a thin strip of wood', and this refers to the strips of wood used to make its rounded body.

The European violin (also called the *kaman/kamanjah* in Arabic). This was adopted into Arab music during the second half of the nineteenth century, replacing an indigenous two-string fiddle that was prevalent in Egypt, also called the *kamanjah*.

The *qanun*. A descendant of the old Egyptian harp, it has played an integral part in Arabic music since the tenth century. The word *qanun* means 'law' in Arabic, and the word exists

---

12   maqamworld.com

in English in the form of 'canon'. The *qanun* was introduced to Europe by the twelfth century, becoming known during the fourteenth to the sixteenth centuries as a psaltery or zither.

The *nay* (Farsi for 'reed'). This is an open-ended, obliquely end-blown flute made of cane. Although very simple, the nay is one of the most difficult Arabic instruments to play. A fine player can produce a large variety of liquid sounds and ornaments; it is an extremely soulful instrument. Its poetical timbre makes it especially suitable for melancholy effects expressing both joy and yearning. It is the only wind instrument used in Arab music, widely appreciated for its warm, breathy sound and its subtle tonal and dynamic inflections.

The *riq* (sometimes called the *daff*). A small tambourine traditionally covered with a goat- or fish-skin head stretched over a wooden frame inlaid with mother-of-pearl. The *riq* has five sets of two pairs of brass cymbals, which produce the exciting jingling sound. The sound of the *riq* sets the rhythm of much Arabic music, particularly in the performances of classical pieces. The *riq* player can single-handedly control the speed and dynamic of an entire orchestra.

One of the most famous Arab singers and public personalities in the twentieth century is the icon and legend Umm Kulthoum.[13] Known also as 'Kawkab al sharq' (star of the East), Umm Kulthoum left an extraordinary collection of religious, sentimental and nationalistic songs that mesmerised audiences from the Arabian Gulf to Morocco. Although her style was influenced by Western popular music of her time, her

---

13 Egyptian singer, born 1904 and died 1975.

music was firmly based in classic Arabic music traditions, and she became known for her emotional, passionate renditions of arrangements by the best composers, poets and songwriters of the day.[14] She always used large orchestras, but the main force in her performances was her own powerful voice. She remained one of the Arab world's best-selling singers even decades after her death. Her songs continue to be frequently heard all over the Arab world.

Another music icon in the Arab world is the Lebanese singer Fairuz[15], who is among the most widely admired and deeply respected living singers in the Arab world. Also known as the 'Jewel of Lebanon' Fairuz sings mostly in her Lebanese dialect and her songs are heard throughout the region.

After Arabic music picked up more Western-style instruments and tones, Arabic pop music spread quickly from Cairo and then Beirut. Sung in either the Egyptian, Lebanese or *khaleeji* (Gulf) dialects, the songs tend to focus on love issues of longing and strife.

Rai is a form of folk music that originated in Algeria from Bedouin shepherds. Mixed with Spanish, French, African and Arabic music forms, this style of music became internationally popular with Cheb Khaled.[16]

Music channels are popular in the region, where some forty channels show Western-style Arabic music videos. Female

14   *Encyclopaedia Britannica.*

15   Lebanese singer born 1935.

16   An Algerian Rai singer and song writer, also known as the King of Rai.

singers are often criticised for their suggestive dancing and scant clothing in these videos.

DANCE

Belly dancing/*Raqs sharqi*. The origins of this style of dancing are not very clear. Made popular in Egypt, belly dancing in the Arab world has two contexts: it is either a performance art, or a social dance that ordinary people perform during celebrations and happy occasions such as weddings and parties while wearing their regular clothes. At these festive social occasions, both men and women of all ages can dance together.

As a performance art, the dancer wears a special costume that emphasises the movement of the hips and belly and the dance focuses more on stagecraft and the use of space. Among the most famous performers in belly dancing are the Egyptian Tahiya Karyouka[17], Fifi Abdo[18] and Najwa Fouad.[19]

Dabkeh is an Arab folk circle and line dance that is popular in Lebanon, Syria, Jordan and Palestine, and also in Iraq and the northern region of Saudi Arabia. Each country has its own variation of the *dabkeh* and the songs that are sung during the dance, but the basic rhythm remains the same. The *dabkeh* is performed by both men and women and, like belly dancing, *dabkeh* is performed by guests at weddings and celebrations and can also be performed by professionals on stage. The line of dancers is formed from right to left and the leader of the

---

17 Egyptian belly dancer and film actress. Born in 1919 and died in September 1999.

18 Egyptian belly dancer, born in 1953.

19 Egyptian belly dancer, born in 1943.

dabkeh heads the line, alternating between facing the audience and the other dancers.

In all the Arabic dances, the audience participates fully in the performance, clapping and singing along with the music.

Hair dancing. This traditional dance is specific to the Arabian Gulf region. A woman loosens her hair and swings her loosened tresses to the right, then left, until she has reached the point that her long tresses can perform figures-of-eight behind her head. A Bedouin woman's long, thick, black hair is considered a valuable sign of beauty.

The dances are performed in pairs or groups, unless specific choreography is designed for a staged performance. Sometimes dancers mirror each other, with one leading. Sometimes they totally ignore each other and dance as if they are alone. In the conservative societies of the Gulf, weddings and celebrations are segregated and so these dances are performed only in the presence of other women – unless it is a staged performance.

Sword dance. This is a traditional Bedouin dance that is popular in the Gulf region. Known in Saudi Arabia as the *ardha*, it involves a group of male dancers carrying swords (or rifles) standing in two lines or a circle, with a poet singing in their midst while they move to the beat of drums and the *rababah*.[20]

---

20   An Arabic musical instrument close to a three-string fiddle.

POETRY

'No people in the world manifest such enthusiastic admiration for literary expression and are so moved by the word, spoken or written, as the Arabs. Modern audiences in Baghdad, Damascus and Cairo can be stirred to the highest degree by the recital of poems, only vaguely comprehended, and by the delivery of orations in the classical tongue, though it be only partially understood. The rhythm, the rhyme, the music, produce on them the effect of what they call "lawful magic" (*sihr halal*).'[21]

Poetry has long been considered one of the highest expressions of literary art in the Arab world. In the days when the Bedouin were constantly travelling, poetry was primarily an oral tradition. People would gather around a storyteller, who would spin tales of love, bravery, chivalry, war and historic events. It was for both entertainment and a way to preserve social traditions and record history. The Holy Quran also took the Arab love of language and poetry to new levels and was considered by many as the ultimate literary model.

The quest for independence and the creation of the state of Israel were two political factors that, along with many others, stimulated a cry for a more 'committed' approach to poetry and literature. During the second half of the twentieth century, the Palestinian people were a continuing source of inspiration for politically committed poets across the Arab world.[22] Mahmoud Darweesh was one such poet, whose lengthy career continued into the twenty-first century. Other poets, such as

21 Philip K. Hitti, *History of the Arabs*.

22 *Encyclopaedia Britannica*.

the Iraqi Abd al Wahhab al Bayati, expressed their commitment to the cause of revolutionary change in other parts of the Arab world, which led Bayati, like so many other modern Arab poets, to live in exile far from his homeland.[23]

Poetry remains very popular today among the Arabs; people frequently gather at poetry and heritage festivals to listen to poets recite in their colloquial dialects and also compete in a number of popular televised poetry competitions.

ART
The teachings of Islam, which view the depiction of the human figure as unholy, have significantly shaped art in the Arab world. Calligraphy, therefore, became the acceptable alternative form of art and the ultimate expression of God's words. However, since the late twentieth century, Western-style paintings and sculptures have become popular, while many countries are also seeing a revival of their more traditional forms of art.

Art galleries and exhibitions are regularly held across the major cities of the Arab world, and many Arab artists have had their work displayed in galleries in Europe and the US.

23 *Encyclopedia Britannica*

BEFORE YOU GO

Don't forget that you are dealing with people and not cultures, and every individual is different. Throughout this book I have tried to bring out the beliefs, values, and viewpoints that tie the Arab world together – a guide to help you understand the 'why' that lies behind the way things are done. Once you have built this basic understanding then you will know how to enjoy and discover the authentic local traditions that are particular to each Arab country and build rewarding relationships with some really warm and genuine people.

So do not forget that although many generalisations hold true, everyone is different, so you will meet a lot of Arabs who are risk-takers, who don't want a family and who really care about sticking to schedules and getting things done quickly.

I have seen a lot of organisations across the Arab world that hire expats as internal consultants; these consultants tend to be at the back end of their career and are happy to come out to the Middle East to earn some tax-free money for a few years. In many cases these are simply the wrong people, here for the wrong reasons. They bring with them a lot of experience but also a lot of baggage – they are absolutely determined as to the way things *should* be done and they want to *teach* the locals and change everything. But of course things don't work this way.

'I have seen companies many times bring in the wrong person. We have had office managers and vice-presidents invite customers to a whisky-tasting evening – in the Gulf countries, where they are all Muslims,' says Saif. 'There are a lot of very educated and qualified people here that speak perfect English, and Arabic of course, and they are from the culture.'

Here are some last words of advice from some of the people I have spoken to…

James Thomas: 'Read and understand as much as you can about the history and the background of the place. When you get there, listen and watch and see how things work before trying to kick up a big storm. And once you have spent time figuring out who the movers and shakers are and how it works and all the rest of it, and played yourself into it, then you can start to influence it by example and through connections in your network as opposed to just storming through the door and believing you can just bash everyone and make a change. It's just not going to happen and you are going to end up being frustrated and then you are going to end up either staying frustrated or leaving.'

Toshihiro Abe: 'Understanding the history is a very important key to knowing how to behave and how to work with the different Arab countries. You must understand which countries were dominated or occupied by the French and which by the English or the Italians – this will give you an understanding of the influences that still exist. History is very important.'

David: 'Set aside your preconceptions and have an open, not defensive mindset, and invest in the relationships. Take the trouble to get beneath the skin of the Arab world – it is quite complicated and there is a huge diversity of people and belief systems – you have to go to people on their terms to really appreciate them – but then it is extremely rewarding.'

Giovanna Negretti: 'Be very patient and open your eyes and ears to understand and to learn why, and don't be quick to jump to conclusions. I am still learning. It's important to come with an open mind and know that things will be different.'

Jonghee Son: 'Acceptance. There is a reason why things are done this way. There is no wrong and right; this is the way it is, it is just different. You have to respect that. A garden is so much more beautiful with many different flowers. Only one flower in the garden – no matter how beautiful – is not so nice.'

Eric: 'The key words here are: relationships; trust and respect. That is a theme across the Arab world. Don't ever pass judgement on what you see, there is a reason why things happen the way they happen; get to understand it, enjoy the learning and you will do much better.'

Peter Millet: 'Remember the importance of dignity and honour. I think it is at the heart of the culture. Therefore, it should be at the heart of the way you approach people. And be aware of the history that you carry with you that may be negatively perceived in some Arab countries.'

Tony Goldner: 'Do a lot more listening than talking. And a lot more observation than judging. You can learn a lot by watching what's happening in a room full of people. I think that's true of anywhere, but you have to understand those dynamics here or just too much doesn't make sense.'

Alexis McGinness: 'Be humble. Be quiet at first and just observe, because that is how you get to see how things work. Then try to adapt as you observe.'

Tari Lang: 'There is a very close relationship between doing business and having personal engagement in the Arab world. Arabs are incredibly warm and friendly. So if you want to work there, you have to really feel you want to work there and enjoy it. Even with all the frustrations, I do love it and I do find it very fulfilling because I do feel that things can move forward quite effectively.'

Sally Zhang: 'Most Chinese are afraid of coming here because of the language problems, because not many Chinese speak English. So they need to find a trusted Arab friend who would help them.'

Peter Millet: 'Learn a bit of the language if you can. It's not easy, but being able to speak a bit of Arabic was very helpful when I visited places outside the capital Amman. It has made a difference. It has enabled people to feel that I respect them that I have made the effort to learn their language.'

Chen Yi Xuan: 'Relax! Enjoy the life. Even if you think it is very slow here – but that is because you have got too much pressure in China. You need to relax and enjoy the time and do whatever you like to do.'

Giovanna Negretti: 'You can have the expat experience and that's fine, but I would urge anyone to have the local experience. To talk more to locals, to get involved in their daily lives, to become friends with them and to live the life that they live, otherwise you would be missing out on an enormous opportunity to meet wonderful people. Wonderful and interesting people who will give you a different perception of what it is to be from here. That's why we go to different places – to learn.'

James Thomas: 'Your experience and your social world is entirely up to you. I have seen more live music, been to more galleries since I lived in Dubai than I did when I lived in London. You have just got to get out and find it. It doesn't throw itself in your face. So go and make an effort: whatever hobby you have got, reengage with it, it will plug you within a social group.'

Dan Monaghan: 'I know a lot of expats who have lived in Dubai for eight years but have never met an Arab, they have never socialised with an Arab, they didn't even understand what Arabic food is, they don't know even the basics about the country they lived in for eight years. They have existed in this bubble of expat life. Why come here if you are just going to go to Costa or Starbucks every week? I would say completely immerse yourself in the culture. And get to really truly understand it, because if you don't, you are missing out on a lot. The more you understand, the more you will enjoy these countries. Don't just scratch the surface, really dig in and get to know the culture. If you dig deep you will find the gems.'

Araz Mahserijian, a business manager from Armenia: 'Get to know the Arabs and interact with them; you will find that there is a lot you can learn. Arabs were leaders in a lot of fields and the rest of the world took what the Arabs started and then developed it. Do not underestimate the Arabs – you can learn a lot here.'

David: 'Do not let anyone tell you that *ta'amiyah*[1] is the same as falafel. If you really want falafel you have to go to Amman or Jerusalem. In Cairo you should just focus on *bamyeh*[2], *mulukhiyah*[3] and *ful*.'

---

1   A kind of food that is made from a mixture of fava beans, parsley and spices, shaped into balls and deep-fried in oil. It is very similar to falafel which is very popular in the Levant countries.

2   Okra cooked usually with tomato sauce, garlic and lamb.

3   A popular green soup made from finely chopped jute leaves. Garlic fried with coriander is added to *mulukhiyah*, and also chicken or rabbit.

APPENDIX:

THE MOST POPULAR DISHES IN THE

ARAB WORLD

Name of the dish	Country where it is most popular	What it consists of
Aseed	Yemen	A mixture of water, salt and flour that is made into a dough, cooked and eaten with gravy. Dried fish can also be added. The dough can also be eaten as dessert by adding sugar and butter or a sweet date mixture.
Baqlawa	Syria, Lebanon, Jordan and Palestine	A rich, sweet pastry made of layers of filo filled with chopped nuts (pistachio, walnuts or pine nuts) and sweetened with syrup or honey.
Basbousah	Egypt and most of the Arab world	A sweet cake made of cooked semolina soaked in simple syrup. Shredded coconut is sometimes sprinkled on top. *Basbousah* is the Egyptian name; it is also known as *hareese* in the Levant.

Couscous	Tunisia, Algeria, Morocco	A traditional Berber dish made from steamed granules of durum wheat. It is served with a meat or vegetable stew spooned over it.
Falafel	Jordan, Palestine, Lebanon and Syria	A ball made from chickpeas, fava beans and various spices, then deep-fried. It can be eaten for breakfast, lunch or dinner. It is served either on a plate or in a pita bread wrap with hommos and taheena.
Fool medames	Egypt, Jordan, Syria, Lebanon and Palestine	*Fool medames*, or simply *fool*, is made of cooked fava beans served with vegetable oil, cumin, and optionally with chopped parsley, garlic, onion, lemon juice and chili pepper. The taste will slightly differ from one country to the other.
Harees	Qatar, UAE, Saudi Arabia	Made from soaked, coarsely ground wheat (consistency of porridge) and usually mixed with chicken. Local variations add different spices.
Hareeseh	Jordan, Lebanon, Syria and Palestine	See *Basbousah*.

Harira	Morocco, Algeria	A traditional soup made from flour, tomatoes, lentils, chickpeas, rice, herbs, lamb or chicken and olive oil.
Kabsa	Saudi Arabia, Kuwait, Bahrain, Qatar, Iraq	Also known as *machbous*, this dish is made from basmati rice, a mixture of spices, with lamb, goat, chicken, fish or shrimp and garnished with roasted pine nuts, almonds and raisins. It is served with a tomato sauce.
Kibbeh or *kubbeh*	Lebanon, Syria, Palestine and Jordan	Its most popular form is a small ball – shaped like an American football – made from cracked wheat, finely minced onions, and finely minced lean lamb or beef meat, then stuffed with minced meat and deep-fried.
Kofta	Most of the Arab world	Minced lamb meat mixed with spices, onions and parsley and shaped into long rolls and then grilled. Served over rice or with hommos or in a sandwich.

Koshari	Egypt	Made from rice, macaroni and lentils, mixed together, topped with a tomato vinegar sauce and garnished with noodles, chickpeas and crispy fried onions.
Kunafeh (*knafeh*, *kanafeh*)	Palestine, Jordan, Syria and Lebanon	A very popular sweet made from a stretchy white cheese (similar to mozzarella) with a topping of rich semolina pastry, all of it soaked in sweet rosewater syrup, garnished with some crushed pistachio nuts.
Labaneh	Lebanon, Jordan, Syria, Palestine.	A creamy yogurt-like spread made from sheep's milk; eaten with bread, usually for breakfast, but also as part of a mezze.
Machbous	Saudi Arabia, Kuwait, Bahrain, Qatar, Iraq	See *kabsa*
Manaqeesh za'atar	Lebanon, Syria, Jordan, Palestine	A pizza with za'atar (a kind of oregano) and olive oil. *Manaqeesh* can also be made with Arabic cheese.

Mandi	Yemen and the Arabian Peninsula	The uniqueness of this dish is in the way the meat is cooked using a special oven called a *tandoor*. A *tandoor* is a hole in the ground covered on the inside with clay. Wood is burned inside until in turns to charcoal. The meat is suspended inside without touching the charcoal, the whole tandoor is then closed to keep all the smoke trapped inside. The meat is served over rice and garnished with raisins and nuts.
Mansaf	Jordan	Served in a large communal dish, pieces of lamb meat served over yellow rice garnished with roasted pine nuts and almonds and soaked with a sauce called *jameed*, made from dried sheep's milk.
Masgouf	Iraq	A traditional dish in Iraq. The fish is cut open in two identical halves from the belly, basted in olive oil, salt, turmeric and tamarind. The fish is then cooked near an open fire. The cooking process can take up to three hours, depending on the size of the fish.

Musakhan	Palestine and Jordan	Made of roasted chicken baked with lots of onions, sumac, allspice, saffron, and fried pine nuts served over taboon bread.
Mulukhiyah	Egypt, Palestine and Jordan	*Mulukhiyah* is made from the leaves of jute and corchorus plants that grow in East and North Africa. It is prepared by chopping the leaves with garlic and coriander and cooking it in an animal stock such as chicken, beef or rabbit, and served with bread or rice.
Qatayef	Most of the Arab world	This is served during Ramadan. A sweet dumpling filled with cream, cheese or walnuts then deep-fried or baked and dipped in syrup.
Sayyadiyeh	Lebanon, Jordan and Palestine	Fried or baked fish with rice, spices and crispy fried onions, garnished with roasted nuts and a brown fish sauce.
Shawerma	Most of the Arab world	Meat – lamb, beef, veal or chicken – stacked on a spit that rotates in front of a flame for hours. *Shawerma* in pita bread sandwiches are a popular meal or snack.

Sheesh tawouk	Most of the Arab world	Pieces of boneless chicken marinated in spices, lemon and garlic, and grilled using skewers. Served as a dish with either rice or hommos, or in a sandwich.
Tajine	The Arab Maghreb	The dish is named after the earthenware pot in which it is cooked. Moroccan *tajine* dishes are slow-cooked savoury stews, typically made with sliced meat, poultry or fish, together with vegetables or fruit. Spices, nuts, and dried fruits are also used.
Umm Ali	Egypt and most of the Arab world	An Egyptian version of bread pudding with cream and pine nuts.
Waraq enab	The Levant	Stuffed vine leaves. The vegetarian version is eaten cold as part of the mezze. The other version is stuffed with rice and minced meat and is eaten hot along with stuffed zucchini.

INDEX

ABOUT THE AUTHOR

Rana Nejem began her career as a broadcast journalist with Jordan Television. After working with CNN during the First Gulf War, she moved to the Royal Hashemite Court, where she was responsible for His Majesty the late King Hussein's international media department for two years. She then moved into the field of communications and public relations, leading the public diplomacy and communications work of the British Embassy in Amman for eighteen years.

In 2013, Rana founded her own company, Yarnu – an Arabic word meaning to look towards, to aspire to, with calmness and serenity. Rana has since been coaching, training and advising business executives, diplomats and officials, helping them refine their professional profile, increase the impact of their personal presence and raise their cultural intelligence. Rana is regularly invited to speak on the subject of cross-cultural communications and cultural intelligence.

Rana has a masters degree in international communications and negotiations from the Fletcher School of Law and Diplomacy in the US, and is a trained coach in inter-cultural intelligence.